Stuart Mansion
Charleston
South Carolina

Built circa 1770 by
Col. John Stuart, his
Majesty's Supt. of Indian
Affairs. A Tory to
his death in 1779

History

This is supposed to be the House from the second story window of which Gen. Francis Marion jumped & broke his leg; a short time afterwards when Charleston was invested by the British Troops, all helpless & infirm people were sent out of the city by the defenders; among these was Gen. Marion; this was fortunate for the Colonial cause, as Marion, known as the "Swamp Fox," recovered & returned to his command to harass the British Troops.

Photograph by Samuel H. Gottscho

H. J. Pringle del.

GREAT GEORGIAN HOUSES *of* AMERICA

Published *for the* Benefit

of the

ARCHITECTS' EMERGENCY COMMITTEE

by the

EDITORIAL COMMITTEE

and the

PUBLICATION COMMITTEE

in two volumes

VOLUME II

DOVER PUBLICATIONS, INC., NEW YORK

Published in Canada by General Publishing Company, Ltd., 30 Lesmill Road, Don Mills, Toronto, Ontario.
Published in the United Kingdom by Constable and Company, Ltd., 10 Orange Street, London WC 2.

This Dover edition, first published in 1970, is an unabridged republication of the work originally published by The Editorial Committee of The Great Georgian Houses of America for the benefit of The Architects' Emergency Committee, and printed as follows: Volume I in 1933 by The Kalkhoff Press, Inc., New York; Volume II in 1937 by The Scribner Press, New York.

Standard Book Number: 486-22492-9
Library of Congress Catalog Card Number: 71-105663

Manufactured in the United States of America
Dover Publications, Inc.
180 Varick Street
New York, N.Y. 10014

TABLE OF CONTENTS

PREFACE

THE Editorial Committee in compiling the present volume, as a continuation of the material published in the first volume of *Great Georgian Houses of America*, has taken a different point of view in making selections for this book. First, the word "Great" has been used in the sense of excellence of design rather than as an indication of the size of the houses. After completing the first volume a large amount of material of fine quality which had been gathered by this committee remained unused. This material represented, in general, houses smaller in size but more varied in plan, in style and in detail and has formed the nucleus for this volume and has determined its character. The word "Georgian" has been given a broader meaning indicating the various phases of style that fall within the reigns of the Four Georges and the intervening Regency.

The object in publishing these volumes was to give work to draughtsmen thrown out of employment in the recent difficult years and in so doing improving their morale, giving them training in an exact and serious technique and rendering financial aid. It has been a great pleasure to this committee to see that many of these men joining in this work did so with great enthusiasm and to find that from being in a state of discouragement, with all its attendant ills, new courage, energy and happiness were the result.

This committee has made it a policy to give employment to all men making application irrespective of their experience in this type of drawing. Many were well qualified and experienced while others needed much coaching. While this training was valuable to all from the educational and technical points of view it was particularly useful to those whose training had been more on commercial and less on artistic lines.

In brief we wish to report that one hundred and ten different men have been given employment in the period from 1932 to 1937 and that this represents nineteen thousand, two hundred and one work hours during this time. The first edition of two thousand volumes is almost exhausted and all the funds from these two volumes have been expended on this object without paying any profit or overhead outside of the actual costs of publishing and mailing.

This committee wishes to thank the subscribers to these volumes and the public for its generous support, those who have permitted the publication of their houses and those who have assisted in procuring the material.

Wm. Lawrence Bottomley

Abbott, Mr. Gordon
Abbott, Mr. Hunley
Ackerman, Arthur & Sons
Adams, Mr. Frederick B.
Adams and Prentice
Addison Gallery of American Art, Phillips Academy
Adler, Miss Blanche
Adler, Mr. David
Aldrich, Mrs. Winthrop W.
Alger, Mrs. Russell A.
Allen, Mrs. Frederick
Alsop, Mr. H. T.
Altschul, Mrs. Frank
American Gallery of Art
Appleget, Mr. Thomas B.
Architectural League of the Western Reserve
Arrington, Mrs. Peter
Artley, Mr. W. H.
Astor, Mrs. Vincent
Auchincloss, Mr. Charles C.
Auchincloss, Mrs. Hugh D.
Auerbach, Mrs. John Hone
Ayer, Mr. W. B.

Babcock, Mrs. Richard
Babcock, Mrs. Woodward
Bacon, Mrs. Robert
Bailey, Mrs. Theodore L.
Baker, Mr. F. C.
Ball, Mr. Thomas Raymond
Barbour, Mrs. W. Warren
Barclay, Mr. H. W.
Barnes, Mr. Charles D.
Barnes, Miss Grace E.
Bartlett, Mrs. Philip G.
Batsford, B. T., Ltd.
Baum, Mr. Dwight James
Beach, Mrs. T. Belknap
Beale, Mrs. Truxtun
Beard, Mr. William Lemen
Berrien, Mrs. Frank D.
Berwind, Mrs. John E.
Bigelow, Mrs. Ruth Campbell
Biggers, Mr. Jas. J. W.
Black & Boyd Mfg. Co.
Bliss, Miss Susan D.
Bloomingdale, Mrs. L. M.
Blow, Mr. George Waller
Bodman, Mr. Herbert L.
Boltimore, Mrs. W. G.
Boncompagnie, Princess Margaret
Bonsal, Mrs. Stephen
Booker, Mrs. N. J.
Boone, Mr. J. R. Herbert
Bossom, Mr. Alfred C., M.P.
Boston Athenaeum Library
Boston Public Library
Bostwick, Mr. A. C.
Bostwick, Mr. D. W.
Bottomley, Mrs. Wm. Lawrence
Bottomley, Mr. Wm. Lawrence
Branch, Mrs. John Kerr
Brewster, Mrs. Frederick F.
Brewster, Mrs. Robert S.
Brinckerhoff, Mr. A. F.
Brixey, Mrs. Richard de Wolf
Bronson, Mrs. J. Hobart
Brown, Mrs. Donaldson
Brown, Mr. Horace
Brown, Mrs. John Nicholas
Brown, Mrs. Lathrop
Bruce, Mrs. William Cabell
Bucknall, Mrs. Henry W. J.
Bulkley, Mrs. Jonathan
Burden, Mr. William A. M.
Burlingham, Mr. Charles C.

Burlingham, Miss A. H.
Burnham Library of Architecture, Art Institute of Chicago
Burton, Mr. H. P.
Buttfield, Mr. Bruce
Byrne, Miss Phyllis

Cabell, Mrs. Robert Gamble, III
Caldwell, Edw. F. and Co., Inc.
Callais, Mr. John
Camp, Mrs. Frederic E.
Cannon, Mrs. Henry White
Carle, Mr. Robert W.
Carnegie Library of Pittsburgh
Carrere, Miss A. M.
Cary, Mrs. Guy
Casey, Mr. Edward
Casselberry, Mrs. Clarence M.
Castle, Mr. W. R.
Century Association, The
Chadwick, Mrs. E. Gerry
Chapman, Mr. Grosvenor
Chase, Miss Edith M.
Chicago Public Library
Choate, Mrs. Arthur Osgood
Choate, Miss Mabel
City Library of Manchester
Claiborne and Taylor, Inc.
Clark, Mr. Gaylord Lee
Clark, Mrs. Julian B.
Clark, Mrs. Stephen C.
Cleveland Museum of Art
Clopton, Dr. Malverne B.
Cluett, Mrs. George A.
Cochran, Mrs. Edwin P.
Cochran, Mrs. Wm. F.
Codman, Mr. Ogden
Coe, Mr. W. R.
Coggeshall, Mary-Jeannette Jukes, Inc.
Colean, Mr. Miles L.
Collins, Mr. Fletcher
Columbia University Library
Cooke, Mrs. Richard A.
Coolidge, Mr. T. Jefferson
Copeland, Mr. Lammot du Pont
Cornell University Library
Corning, Miss Anne
Cowles, Mr. Wm. Sheffield
Cox, Mrs. Attilla
Crane, Mr. Donald F.
Cravath, Mr. Paul D.
Crisp, Mr. H. G. and Mr. J. R. Edmunds, Jr.
Crocker, Mr. Frank L.
Cromwell, Mrs. Lincoln
Crosley, Mr. Powell, Jr.
Crowninshield, Mrs. F. B.
Cunningham, Mr. John J., Jr.
Currier Gallery of Art
Cushing, Mrs. Charles
Cutting, Mrs. W. Bayard

Dalton, Mr. Robert
Dana, Mrs. R. H.
Danforth, Mrs. Murray S.
Daniel, Mr. Robert W.
D'Arcy, Mrs. Paul
David, Mr. Donald K.
Davie, Mrs. Preston
Davis, Mr. Walter G.
Davison, Mrs. Henry P.
Dawes, Mr. Dexter B.
DeBevoise, Mr. George
DeCuevas, Mr. George
Defrees, Mr. Donald
DeGroote, Mr. Karl
Delafield, Gen. John Ross
DeLagerberg, Mr. Guy

Delano & Aldrich
Delehanty, Mr. Bradley
Dixon, Mr. W. Palmer
Dodge, Mr. Donald D.
Dominick, Mrs. G. G.
Donaldson, Mrs. John W.
Donn, Mr. Edward W., Jr.
Du Bose, Mr. D. St. Pierre
Du Moulin, Mrs. R. K.
Dunbaugh, Mr. George J.
du Pont, Mrs. Alfred I.

Edell, Miss Alberta C.
Edey, Miss Louise
Edmonds, Mrs. John Worth
Elkins, Mr. W. M.
Ellis, Mrs. Ralph
Ellsworth, Mrs. J. Magee
Elton, Mr. John P.
Ely, Mr. Albert H., Jr.
Ely, Mr. Wilson C.
Embury, Mr. Aymar, II
Endicott, Mr. & Mrs. Wm. C.
Ensign, Mrs. Joseph P.
Esberg, Mrs. Henry
Esberg, Mr. Henry
Eshleman, Mr. I. Stauffer
Eustis, Mrs. W. C.
Evans, Mrs. Henry
Ewing, Mrs. William

Falk, Mr. Myron S.
Farnam, Mrs. Tracy
Farr, Daniel H., Company
Farrand, Mr. Max
Fauber and Poston
Fernschild, Mr. George J., Jr.
Ferry, Mrs. Mansfield
Ferry, Mrs. Ronald M.
Field, Mrs. E. Marshall
Fisher, Mr. D. K. Este
Fisher, Mr. L. McLane
Fisher, Mr. Samuel H.
Fisher, Mrs. William A.
Flagler, Mrs. H. H.
Flagler, Mr. H. H.
Ford Motor Company Library
Forster, Mr. Frank J.
Fowler, Mr. Laurence Hall
Francis, Mrs. G. Tappan
Franklin, Mrs. George S.
Freedlander, Mr. Joseph R.
Frelinghuysen, Mr. P. H. B.
French and Co., Inc.
Frick, Miss Anne T.
Frick, Mr. Childs
Froehlinger, Mr. Richard A.

Gade, Mrs. John A.
Gallatin, Mr. Albert Eugene
Garvan, Mrs. Francis P.
Gates, Mrs. A. L.
Georgia School of Technology
Gibbons, Mrs. John H.
Gibson, Mr. Hamilton
Gibson, Mr. Harvey D.
Gilbert, Mr. S. Parker
Gillette, Mr. Charles F.
Gillie, Mr. James Ross
Glazier, Mrs. Henry S.
Godley, Mr. Frederick A.
Goodrum, Mrs. James J.
Goodwin, Mr. James L.
Goodwin, Mr. Philip L.
Goucher College Library
Gould, Mr. Bruce
Gould, Mrs. Edwin
Greenwood Book Shop, Inc.
Grew, Mr. Randolph C.
Griffin, Mr. William V.

Griswold, Mr. B. Howell, Jr.
Grosvenor, Mr. William G.

Hafner, Mr. Albert
Hagen, Mr. Winston H
Hague, Miss Marion
Hall, Mr. Howard G.
Hall, Mr. Perry E.
Hall, Mr. Weeks
Halle, Mr. H. J.
Halsey, Mr. R. T. H.
Hamilton, Mr. Edward P.
Hamilton, Mr. John G.
Hamilton, Mr. William H.
Hamlen, Mrs. Paul N.
Hammond, Mrs. John Henry
Haneman, Mr. John Theodore
Hardon, Mrs. Henry W.
Harkness, Mrs. Edward S.
Harlan, Miss Laura
Harris, Mrs. Basil
Harrison, Mrs. Jennie G. D.
Harrison, Mrs. Joseph Duke
Hartford, Mrs. E. V.
Harvard College Library
Harvard Cooperative Society
Haskell, Mrs. J. Amory
Hasslacher, Mrs. George F.
Hawkes, Mrs. Forbes
Hawley, Miss Theodosia deR.
Hay, Mrs. Clarence L.
Hayes, Mrs. James H.
Hegeman, Miss Annie May
Helburn, Mr. Morris
Helburn, Mr. William
Heller, Mr. Robert H.
Henry, Mr. Seton
Hepburn, M.P., Mr. Patrick Buchan
Herter, Mr. Albert
Hewitt, Mr. Edward S.
Heyward, Mr. Henderson
Higgins, Mr. Charles H.
Hill, James Jerome, Reference Library
Hines, Mrs. Walker D.
Hodgdon, Mr. Frederick C.
Hoff, Mrs. Charles
Holland, Mr. Julian
Holliday Bookshop, The
Holmes, Mr. Gerald A.
Holmes, Oliver Wendell, Library, Phillips Academy
Hooper, Mrs. Harriet
Hopkins, Mr. D. Luke
Hopkins, Mrs. Robert D.
Hopkins University, Johns
Hornblower, Mrs. George S.
Houghton, Mr. Arthur A., Jr.
Housatonuc Bookshop
Howard, Mrs. George
Howells, Mrs. John Mead
Hoyt, Mr. Charles B.
Humphrey, Mrs. Lewis C.
Huntington Library, Henry E., San Marino, Calif.
Huszagh, Mr. Lyman Peyton
Hutchins, Mrs. Edward W.
Hutzler Bros.
Hyde, Mrs. Louis F.

Indiana State Library
Ingraham, Mr. Edward
Ireland, Miss Elisabeth
Irvin, Mr. Willis
Iselin, Mrs. Lewis
Iselin, Miss Louise M.
Iselin, Mrs. O'Donnell

James, Mrs. Bayard

James, Mrs. Oliver B.
Jamison, Mr. T. Worth, Jr.
Jarvie, Miss A. F. G.
Jennings, Miss Annie Burr
Jennings, Mr. Oliver B.
Johns Hopkins University
Johnson, Mrs. Robert Wood
Johnson, Mr. Robert W.
Johnson, Mrs. Terrell
Johnston, Mrs. Edith Newlands
Jones and Erwin, Inc.
Jones, Miss Evelyn B.
Jones, Mrs. Marion Telva
Jones, Mr. Robert E.
Junior League Circulating
   Library, Washington, D. C.
Juta, Mr. Jan

Kahn, Mr. Ely Jacques
Kahn, Mrs. Otto H.
Kansas Library, University of
Kean, Mrs. John
Kelley, Mrs. Nicholas
Kennedy, Mrs. J. Foster
Ketcham, Mr. Walter S.
Kilbreth, Mr. J. William
Kimbel, A., & Son, Inc.
Kingsbury, Miss Alice E.
Kingsbury, Col. Howard Thayer
Knight, Mrs. Webster
Knowlton, Mr. Eben B.
Koebler, Mr. William G.

LaBeaume, Mr. Louis
Labrot, Mr. S. W.
Ladd, Mrs. William S.
LaGatta, Mr. John
Lagerberg, Mr. Lars de
Laird, Mr. Philip D.
Lambert, Mr. Gerald B.
Lamhill, Mr. Richard V. A.
Lancashire, Mrs. J. Henry
Landon, Mr. Harold M.
Landsman, Mr. Samuel
Langdon, Miss Helen
Lanier, Mrs. Charles D.
Lashin, Mr. Nathan A.
Laughlin, Miss Gertrude
Lee, Arthur H., and Sons, Inc.
Lee, Mr. Cazenove G., Jr.
Lefferts, Mrs. Barent
Leidy, Mrs. C. F.
Leonard, Mrs. Henry
Levi, Mr. Julian Clarence
Lewis, Mr. Wadsworth R.
Lewis, Mrs. Wilmarth S.
Lindsay, Sir Ronald and Lady
Littlejohn, Mrs. Robert M.
Livingston, Mr. Goodhue
Livingston, Mrs. John H.
Lloyd, Mrs. Horatio G.
Lloyd-Smith, Mrs. Wilton
Lockwood, Mr. Luke Vincent
Long, Mrs. Breckenridge
Long, Mr. Maurice Alvin
Lopez, Mrs. J. E.
Lounsberry, Miss Alice
Luce, Mr. and Mrs. Stephen B.
Ludowici-Celadon Co.
Lyman, Miss Mabel

MacCracken, Mrs. George
MacKenzie, Mr. James C.
McConnell, Mrs. James Eli
McKim, Mead and White
McKim, Mr. Robert V.
McLane, Mrs. Allan, Jr.
McMillan, Mr. William
McMillen, Inc.
Machen, Mr. Thomas
Magruder, Miss Evelina
Marburg, Miss Emma
Marsalis, Mrs. Thomas
Marsh, Miss E. Mabel

Mason, Mr. Elliott B.
Mason, Mr. Eugene Waterman
Massie, Mrs. William R.
Mathews, Mr. Edward J.
Maxwell, Miss J. Alice
Maynard, Mrs. Walter E.
Melchers, Mrs. Gari
Meltzer, Mr. Herman
Mercer, Mrs. William R.
Merle-Smith, Mrs. Kate F.
Merrell, Miss Elenor
Merrill, Mrs. Keith
Merrill, Mr. Keith
Metcalf, Mrs. Jesse H.
Metropolitan Museum of Art
Meyer, Mr. Eugene
Milbank, Mrs. Jeremiah
Milliken, Mr. Henry Oothout
Minnesota, University of
Moffat, Frank Everest, Inc.
Moffatt, Mrs. R. Burnham
Monroe, Mrs. Robert G.
Moore, Mr. Benjamin
Moore, Mrs. Edward S.
Moore, Mr. Frederic P.
Moore, Mrs. Paul
Morgan, Mr. H. S.
Morgan, Mrs. John Hill
Morgan, Mr. Junius S.
Morgan, Mr. Lancaster
Morgan, Shirley W.
Morgan, Mr. William Fellowes
Morris, Mr. Benjamin Wister
Morris, Mr. Froome
Morris, Mrs. George Maurice
Morris, Mrs. Lewis S.
Morrow, Mrs. Dwight W.
Morss, Mrs. Everett
Moseley, Mr. Fred S., Jr.
Munson, Mr. Charles S.
Museum of Fine Arts Library,
   Boston

Nash, Mrs. Ogden
National Geographical Society
Newton, Mr. Francis
New York Public Library
New York School of Interior
   Decoration
Nichols, Mrs. George
Nielson, Mrs. Joseph L.
Noland, Miss Charlotte H.
Norton, Mrs. C. D.
Norton, Mrs. G. W.
Norton, Mr. L. A.
Noyes, Mr. Laurence G.
Noyes, Mrs. R. B.

Oberlin College
O'Dwyer, Mr. David W.
O'Dwyer, Mr. Edward F.
Olds, Mr. Irving S.
Osborn, Mr. William Church

Parks, Mrs. Elton
Paskus, Mrs. Benjamin G.
Patterson, Mr. Jefferson
Patterson, Mrs. J. M.
Payson, Mrs. Charles S.
Payson, Mr. Herbert
Payson, Mr. Phillips M.
Pell, Mrs. Stephen H.
Pennoyer, Mr. Paul G.
Pennsylvania, University of
Perlman, Mr. Philip B.
Perry, Shaw and Hepburn
Peters, Miss Isabel
Peyton, Mrs. William C.
Philadelphia, Free Library of—
   George S. Pepper Fund
Phillips, Mr. James Duncan
Phillips, Mr. William
Phipps, Mr. Howard
Phipps, Mr. John

Pierrepont, Mrs. Seth Low
Pinger, Mrs. W. H., Jr.
Pittsburgh, University of
Polhemus and Coffin
Pope, Mr. Lester B.
Potter, Mrs. R. Burnside
Pratt, Mrs. Frederic B.
Pratt, Mrs. Frederic R.
Pratt, Mr. George D.
Pratt, Mrs. John T.
Pratt Institute Free Library
Pratt Institute (School of Fine
   and Applied Arts)
Prentice, Mrs. John H.
Princeton University
Pringle & Smith
Providence Athenaeum
Provost, Mr. Frederick
Pryibil, Mr. Paul

Rafferty, Mrs. M. G.
Randolph, Mr. Francis F.
Raskob, Mr. John J.
Rawson, Mrs. Hobart
Raymond, Mr. James I.
Redmond, Mrs. Johnston L.
Reed, Mrs. Verner Z., Jr.
Reinhard and Hofmeister
Remington-Putnam Book Co.
Rennie, Miss Louise
Rennolds, Mr. Edmund Addison
Rentschler, Mrs. Gordon S.
Reynolds, Mrs. Jackson R.
Reynolds, Mrs. John
Reynolds, Mr. Kenneth G.
Richardson, Mrs. Alden B.
Riddle, Mrs. Theodate Pope
Riley, Miss Mabel Louise
Rinschede, Mr. Charles A. W.
Rockefeller, Mrs. John D., Jr.
Rockefeller, Mr. Nelson A.
Rodriguez, Professor A. S.
Roebling, Mrs. F. W.
Rogers, Mr. James Gamble
Royal Institute of British
   Architects
Russell, Mr. Charles H.
Russell, Mr. Faris R.
Russell, Mr. T. M.

Satterlee, Mrs. Herbert L.
Schloesing, Mr. Jean
Schmidlapp, Mrs. C. J.
Schofield, Mrs. William H.
Schwab, Miss Katherine P.
Scoville, Miss Edith
Sears, Miss Evelyn G.
Sebring, Mr. and Mrs. H. O., Jr.
Sedgwick, Mr. Henry R.
Sharpe, Mr. Henry D.
Shaw, Mr. Walter K., Jr.
Sheffield, Mr. Henry E.
Shepherd, Mr. William Edgar
Shipman, Mrs. Ellen
Smart, Mrs. L. Bruce
Smith, Mr. Charles C.
Smith, Dr. E. Terry
Smith, Mr. Francis Palmer
Smith, Mr. Gregory
Smith Library, Hamilton, Uni-
   versity of New Hampshire
Solley, Mrs. Katherine Lilly
Spalding, Mrs. Albert
Sprague, Mrs. Isaac
Stechert, G. E. & Co.
Stern, Mr. Philip N.
Stevens Institute of Technology
Stevens, Mr. Joseph S.
Stevens, Mr. Shepherd
Stewart, Mr. J. Adger
Stillman, Miss Charlotte R.
Stillman, Mr. Chauncey
Stillman, Dr. Edgar
Stout, Mr. Andrew V.

Straus, Mr. Percy S.
Strawbridge, Mrs. R. E., Jr.
Swan, Mrs. T. W.
Swan, Mrs. Thomas W.

Talbot, Mr. J. Alden
Taylor, Mr. Bertrand L., Jr.
Taylor, Mr. Henry Osborne
Tener, Mrs. George E.
Texas, The University of
Thatcher, Mrs. Thomas D.
Thomas, Miss Mabel L. H.
Thomas, Mrs. Samuel Hinds
Thompson, Mr. M. D.
Thoms and Eron, Inc.
Thorne, Mrs. Oakleigh
Ticonderoga Museum, Fort
Tiffany, Mrs. Cameron
Tovell, Mr. C. Eugene
Treadway, Mr. Townsend G.
Treanor & Fatio
Tudor, Mrs. Henry D.
Tyssowski, Mrs. John

Ulrichs, Mr. T. William
University Club Library
Utica Public Library

Valentine Museum, Richmond
Van Name, Miss Theodora
Vauclain, Mr. Samuel
Vaughan, Mrs. Henry G.
Vernay, Arthur S., Inc.
Vickers, Mrs. Reginald J.

Wade, Mr. Edwin J.
Wadsworth, Mrs. Dudley
Wadsworth, Mrs. Lillian
Wagner, Mr. Herbert A.
Walker, Mrs. A. Stewart
Walker, Mr. William H.
Washington, University of
Waterbury, Miss Florence
Watland, Mr. G. R. W.
Watson, Mr. Thos. J.
Webb, Mrs. J. Watson
Webb, Mr. Maurice
Weddell, Mr. Alexander W.
Wells, Mr. John B.
Wenzel, Mr. Paul
White, Mr. Cornelius J.
White, Mr. J. Du Pratt
White, Mrs. Miles, Jr.
Whitney, Mrs. Casper
Whitney, Mrs. George
Whitney, Mrs. Geoffrey G.
Whitney, Miss S. N.
Whitridge, Mrs. Arnold
Whittemore, Miss Gertrude B.
Widener, Mr. George D.
Wild, Miss Rosamund D.
Williams, Mrs. Andrew Murray
Williams, Mrs. George Weems
Williams, Mr. Lynn A.
Winston, Mr. Owen
Winthrop, Mr. Grenville L.
Winthrop, Mrs. Robert
Wise, Mrs. Anderson
Wissmann, Mr. F. DeR.
Wolcott, Mrs. Henry
Wood, Mrs. E. Allan
Wood, Miss Margaret White
Wood, Mrs. Willis D.
Woolsey, Mr. Heathcote M.
Worcester, Mr. Wakefield
Worthington, Mr. Ellicott H.
Wright, Richardson
Wyeth and King

Yale University
Yeatman, Miss Georgina P.

Zinn, Mrs. George

REGIONAL TYPES IN
EARLY AMERICAN ARCHITECTURE

BY FISKE KIMBALL

ARLY American houses, in their relation to corresponding works in England, may be considered in two complementary aspects. On the one hand we may observe their conformity to buildings of equivalent size and date in England, a conformity often very striking, especially in the more ambitious and conspicuous Colonial houses. On the other hand we may emphasize the ways in which they differ from such English precedents, ways by which they become characteristically American. That is what we shall attempt here. We shall find our houses, even those of the scale shown in this book, to be full of interesting regional variety, characteristic, not merely of America, but of the soil and culture of their own colonies and districts.

THE COLONIAL PERIOD

Let us summarize first in a few words the development in England, and the general nature of the development in America, before we turn to the variety that existed in the different regions and colonies. In England, following the Restoration, there were two chief phases, the older inaugurated by the work of Wren. This was much permeated by Dutch influence, which is largely responsible for the preference for brick over stone. It was also influenced by the Italian baroque, with its preference for broken and curved forms, such as the familiar one seen in a sketch of Wren's own for an interior doorway—the broken, scroll pediment. In domestic work of this phase there was usually an elaboration of individual

features rather than any large ordonnance of columns or pilasters.

In contrast with this phase, there came, as the 18th century wore on, the phase influenced by Lord Burlington, who championed the earlier style of Inigo Jones and of the great forerunner of all the academists, Palladio. That involved a struggle to eliminate the baroque features. At the same time, it involved a more monumental treatment and a more conspicuous use of the orders, as we see in Burlington's design for General Wade's house, with the whole front adorned by pilasters. To a minor degree, the same trend prevailed in the interiors, where we find the scroll pediment tending to disappear. Other arbiters of taste, however, sponsored different styles for the interiors. We see the influence of the French work of Louis XV—the *rocaille*—in the drawing-room of Lord Chesterfield, who was the great protagonist of the French style in England, as Burlington was of the "Venetian" and Walpole of the Gothic. French, Gothic and Chinese joined in harmonious rivalry, in such work as the furniture designs of Chippendale.

In America in the 18th century we find those two successive phases, a little later than the work in the British capital, but perhaps not later than in the British provinces. Of course all this represents a great change from the 17th century American work, in substituting for the survival of the medieval features, which had been the outstanding characteristic of the 17th century work, the whole cycle of classical inspiration deriving ultimately from the Italian Renaissance. The influence of English developments had resulted by the year 1725 in reforming the house from one primarily medieval into one of classical elements arranged with formal symmetry, and preoccupied with beauty of form rather than with expression of structure. The Wren phase is represented by such a house as Westover on the James, brick in material, with details of classical cast and baroque character in the scroll pediment. The more monumental, the more academic features later appear. The Apthorpe house in New York was one of the most monumental of these, not perhaps the finest and purest, but the richest in its classical ordonnance. To a certain degree more academic quality appeared in the interior here also. Simultaneously came the adoption, without any sense of incongruity, of the French *rocaille* motives, as in the ornaments and ceiling of the Powel room from Philadelphia now in the Pennsylvania Museum.

So much for the general course of development, before we turn to the individual colonies. We see that the styles which prevailed in England were adopted here very soon after their appearance, and, in the finest houses, with a degree of understanding equal to that of the English provinces. London we could not expect to rival. So far as their best houses were concerned, the thirteen colonies stood very much on the plane of thirteen more shires of rural England, differing from the other shires of England no more than from one another and no more than the English rural shires differed among themselves.

It is not so much in these finer houses, then, that we are to seek the specially characteristic American note. It is rather in the isolated houses where workmen, instead of piquing themselves on a perfect following of the latest London fashion, built forward unconsciously in new directions. These have still greater interest for us because, beside belonging to us as a whole, they belong to various individual localities.

In any attempt to study this variety of the Colonial

work we are still only near the beginnings. It is a vast enterprise and one that we cannot hope to exhaust in a moment. Indeed, we must make several reservations before we rush in too hastily. In the first place, we must emphasize that our local classification cannot be absolutely rigid. Isolated examples of some features might occur almost anywhere, but they are, none the less, especially characteristic of certain regions, and predominate there. These we will make the subject of our study. And, in a similar way, we must recognize that, although we first consider the period before the Revolution, many of the houses of these Colonial types were built after the War. Our interest here is to follow out those types which were characteristic of the different colonies before the Revolution, many of which persisted for a long time.

Let us begin with New England. One cannot define the Colonial characteristics in too minute regions except in special cases, and so we take first New England as a whole. It is full of minor variety, but it has nevertheless a unity as against the rest of the colonies, a unity recognized politically at one time in the "United Colonies of New England." New Hampshire was part of Massachusetts for a brief period; Maine belonged to it until 1820. We recall, first of all, the New England country village with its common, as at Fairfield, or its elm-lined street, as at Deerfield; the fishing village, with its small houses hugging the rocky ledges and winding along narrow streets, as at Marblehead; the farmhouse, perhaps a little bleak, on that barren soil where the first fathers planted their settlements, as at Duxbury.

One of the chief local characteristics in architecture anywhere is the choice of materials. That was notably true in England. The idea that Colonial architecture was chiefly of wood is an idea formed on the New England work, where it was true as in no other section. There were reasons in the Northern latitudes why masonry walls proved very damp, so that masonry was rarely used, and wood was almost universal. The houses were covered, after the first few years, with shingles, as in Nantucket and Plymouth, or with clapboards, usual elsewhere in New England.

Another local characteristic is the general type of mass, the form of the house in the large. Of the types of mass, two important ones were survivals of the 17th century. The most characteristic in New England was the house with the lean-to. This persisted through the 18th century well down into the 19th. Nowhere do we see it better than in the famous Adams houses at Quincy, where we have the houses of father and son side by side, both of the lean-to type, almost identical in their general form. These are normal examples. An extreme one may be seen in the Orton house at Woodbury, Connecticut, so expressive of the snowbound New England winter.

The other type which had its beginnings in the 17th century was the type with the gambrel roof. It was formed by cutting off steep-pointed roofs to prevent them from rising too high, especially as houses became thicker. We find it sometimes on a narrow house, one room in depth, as still at The Lindens, but more often on the thicker house, with double file of rooms, which was characteristic of the 18th century as against the 17th. Nowhere can we see the solid, hospitable lines made by the gambrel roof better than at Old Gate in Farmington.

Nearly related is the cottage with a pitch roof continuing to a simple triangular gable at either end. It had come in along with the classical pediment, but the low gable was employed in New England without overhanging mouldings, the eaves clinging close to the wall.

We should not get a clear picture of the New England house if we did not speak of one feature which was very characteristic of it. Surely any of us who were born in New England have heard of it from our earliest years—the ell. The New England house with its great conservatism, fostered by the early founding of its colonies, tended to remain narrow;

consequently additional room was often provided by another mass at right angles, making an L form for the house as a whole, as, on a great scale, even at Old Gate.

Beyond the ell stretched the shed, another characteristic New England feature. In the South one could have isolated outbuildings. The kitchen was usually separate. Food could be carried in. In New England, where one had to contend with snow and a cold winter, the effort was to make all the dependencies continuous, the sheds extending interminably. It is this very feature which has often caused the destruction of the New England house. The whole went if any part took fire.

As to the interior, I am not sure that a great many features were limited to restricted districts like New England. Nevertheless, it is certainly true that only in New England, and only in Connecticut, would we find a room like the one from Newington, in the Metropolitan Museum, with its cross panels below and its round-headed panels above, and with the particular form, far from canonical, which the pilaster took at the hands of the native carpenter.

The twisted baluster and newel, in their glory, were specially New England features. Not that we do not find them at all elsewhere, but that elsewhere we should scarcely find the three types of differently twisted balusters on each step, repeating again three, three and three, or the newel with the double spiral, twisting inside in one direction and outside in the other. These features were inaugurated, so far as we know, in the Hancock stairway in Boston, and henceforth were duplicated in scores of New England examples right down to the Revolution.

It is to the Hancock house that we trace another feature which has perhaps, more than any other, a local orbit—the Connecticut Valley doorway. I say Connecticut Valley very advisedly, and not Connecticut River. It will be remembered that from Middletown to New Haven there runs an extension of the Connecticut Valley, whereas the river itself turns off in a rather narrow path to the sea at Saybrook. All the way up that broad valley and then up the river from Middletown past the Massachusetts border, we find a particular doorway marked by opposite curved scrolls carried out with the utmost freedom. Why does it appear there and nowhere else? I think the answer is to be found in the fact that the stone for the Hancock house was cut at Middletown, where drawings of it must have been sent for that purpose. The house had, in the second story, a balcony doorway with grouped pilasters, pedestals, and a scroll pediment backed by rustic blocks—exactly the formula which we find in the Connecticut Valley doorway, as in the example from Westfield in the Metropolitan Museum. More than any other feature they show what the carpenter and craftsmen in retired districts did when they were free from the grammatical canons of the orders and could vary their forms in a colloquial way. We see with what freedom the capital, which was once the Corinthian, has been handled.

It is a fascinating study to see just how far these doorways extend, which demonstrates how they cling along the Connecticut Valley, quite irrespective of the state line of Connecticut and Massachusetts.

Some local characteristics were far more restricted in area. In the Deming and Sheldon houses at Litchfield, and in Old Gate at Farmington, there is a type of frontispiece with columns below and a Palladian window above found only in these three neighboring examples.

When we come from New England to New York, we begin to suffer from the growth of this great city, which has constantly destroyed its own offspring. The old Dutch house built in the 17th century, with its stepped gable, ceased to be built about 1700. With the new century, the forms of English 18th century architecture were followed in this colony as much as elsewhere, but they were given here as elsewhere a local tinge producing what is called the "Dutch Colonial." Although some features, like the stoop, were Dutch, not all came from Holland. They were the product of Dutch settlers here. The gambrel roof, for instance, while occasionally found in Holland, is not specifically Dutch. Most of the examples commonly shown represent the style after the Revolution. It is only in the environs that there are remains of the minor pre-Revolutionary work, in east Jersey, up the Hudson, and on Staten Island and on western Long Island. Most individual are the houses of the Hudson Valley, especially in Ulster County, as at Hurley and New Paltz. The houses are of stone, and, whether one or two rooms deep, have their chimneys in the middle of the ends. Their steep gables are often wholly or partly of weatherboards. Most are of a single story, but two-story houses are not uncommon and some of these have a lean-to at the rear. There is no substantial overhang either at the eaves or at the gable.

Around New York the lower gable, and doubtless the gambrel roof, appeared before the Revolution. The Rapalje house at New Lots, Long Island, illustrated the type, and the adoption of very widely overhanging eaves. When supported by light posts these made the piazzas which the painter Copley, unfamiliar with them in Boston, noted in numbers just before the Revolution. The typical covering material was the long shingle. One does not find such shingles in New England, but in western Connecticut and about New York they are characteristic. They extended down Long Island even into a region where the type of house was derived from New England. In little cottages at Patchogue and other towns of eastern Long Island we find the New England coast type covered with the New York material.

None of the Colonial towns had a more pronounced individual character than Philadelphia. In no other have whole streets been preserved to our day such as Cherry Street or Elfreth's Alley in Philadelphia. Some of the features which contributed to this individuality were the brick, and the heavy white wooden shutters, scarcely found in New England.

In Pennsylvania there were, to be sure, a number of different traditions and well-marked types, because the settlers came from various countries. Penn gave his hospitality to all. The Germans or "Pennsylvania Dutch" brought with them certain features which they kept with great tenacity, and produced an architectural dialect, analogous to that in language, which we feel to be characteristically Pennsylvanian. We find this especially at Germantown. Stone or stucco are the usual materials. The house is typically of two stories with broad gables at the ends. There is a wide overhang at the eaves, a long projecting hood above the windows of the ground story, a stoop at the door.

One of the most interesting chapters on Colonial architecture might be written of the buildings of the German sectarians, who settled at Bethlehem, Ephrata, and around Lancaster. It is in their work alone that we find one type of building, the half-timber house with framing exposed on the exterior. The schoolhouse in Oley township is one of the few examples still standing. There were also formerly in Lancaster the Powel house and at least one other, in which there were interesting combinations of brick and half-timber. At Ephrata, the great stronghold of the Dunkards, are monastic buildings still preserving to our day the interesting civilization of the Pennsylvania Dutch of the 18th century. Most striking is the doorway of the Sister House, so different from the conventional conception of what is American. Stucco is the material here. In the interior, furniture and accessories very unlike those of the other colonies mark this particularly interesting local variant.

When we come to the South, we have first of all to consider a little the peculiar character of the Southern civilization. It was very different from that of the North. It was not a commercial civilization dependent on sea-coast towns or on manufacturing, but was purely an agricultural civilization, with the rarest exceptions. The broad river estuaries of the Tidewater permitted vessels to ascend to the planta-

tion wharf, and it was only with the utmost difficulty that the home government was able to encourage the building even of the little Colonial capitals like Williamsburg. There were great baronial plantations which were the true communities of the South, often with hundreds of inhabitants. The population was scattered in these plantation communities, deprived of the continuous services of skilled workmen, and cut off from help in case of fire, which was constantly destroying plantation houses. Then they have suffered far more serious depredations. Virginia was a battleground for four years; South Carolina and Georgia were systematically laid waste. It is a terrible thing to lose in war, when there follows enforced repudiation of national debt and paper. It is surprising that so much is left.

In the South it is only at Charleston that we find really urban types. Even at Annapolis the houses are semi-rural. There, a five-part scheme—with wings and connecting passages, not unknown elsewhere—was particularly characteristic, as in the Brice house. Tuckahoe in Virginia may serve as an example to suggest the character of the plantation establishment: a self-contained unit, with facilities for growing or making most of what it needed, everything that did not have to be ordered directly from London.

When we come down from the great houses to the minor houses, we find first that they are few. During the Colonial period in the South there scarcely was a "middle class." Where we do find a small house, we find it (like the outbuildings of the great mansions) marked by certain peculiarities which seem Southern, even if they are not wholly confined to the South. One of these is the presence of end chimneys. In the New England house, typically, the great chimney rises in the center. In the Virginia and the Maryland houses, the chimneys rise at either end.

When we come to Charleston, we find the town itself unique, with certain features wholly local. Among these is the existence of two types of plan, called there the "single house" and the "double house." The names have nothing to do with the number of families occupying the house. They mean the house one room wide and the house two rooms wide. Both typically have their halls running parallel to the street and are entered at the side from a long veranda. Typical of Charleston, too, is the great development of the walls and gateways, with beautiful wrought iron work, as in the Stuart house, with its characteristic stable court.

THE EARLY REPUBLIC

The Revolution made a great change in the style of American architecture, and not for the worse, as used formerly to be thought. Fifty years ago, with the first revival of interest in things Colonial, it was believed that art died a natural death just about the time of the Revolution, and that the only work we had that was worth attention was the Colonial. The word Colonial, however, was soon extended to include very much that was done after the Revolution. Thus people came gradually to the acceptance, one might almost say under false colors, of the great body of the work of the early Republic which today we are quite as ready to accept under its own true colors. Indeed, the more we study the actual time of origin of the most beautiful products of early American domestic architecture, the more we find that many of those which we supposed were the work of the Colonial day originated after the Revolution. Thus many aspects of what is thought loosely to be "Colonial architecture" will first come before our eyes now as we speak of the earliest work of the Republic.

We have attempted to study elsewhere the chronological evolution of this work, so we shall devote just one general word to that, and then turn to a subject less fully studied, the diversity of local tradition, the regional variety.

The change which took place with the Revolution was, in general, the adoption of a more classical style. That was, to be sure, coming everywhere, but it took in America a particularly pronounced form, owing to the enthusiasm for things Roman and Greek which flowed from the democratic character of the new Republic. It took the ancient republics as models. The sophomoric analogy that was responsible for the numerous examples from Plutarch in the oratory of the time, and for the name of the great patriotic order of the Cincinnati, was responsible also for the ultimate adoption of a literal version of the classical style, unparalleled anywhere in Europe, richly illustrated in this volume.

Jefferson, who had been the author of the declaration of political independence, was the great protagonist of this declaration of artistic independence from contemporary Europe, and the leader of the classical enthusiasts. Ultimately they brought about the adoption of the form of the classical temple, in complete literalness for all classes of buildings—the public building, the church, and even the dwelling. It took two generations from the time of the War, however, for that movement to come to full fruition, even though its germs are to be found in Jefferson's work actually during the course of the Revolutionary struggle. Thus its riper fruits lie outside our subject here, which is the work of the generation immediately following the Revolution, not much beyond the year 1800.

In this work also the novel element was classical, but most of it had not the thorough-going classicism of Jefferson and his followers. It was a classicism in the Pompeian style, fathered in England by the Adam brothers and flourishing also in France under Louis XVI. It was a very fine and delicate version of classical decorative elements, applied to a body not so different from what had gone before.

One or two examples will fix in mind the general character of this Pompeian style of the early Republic, which derived its inspiration from the Adam work in England. Perhaps the most beautiful American room still existing is the ballroom of the Lyman House in Waltham, designed by McIntire, illustrated in the first volume of this title. With the great elongation of the columns and delicacy of the stucco ornaments, it admirably exemplifies the essential character of this style—the delicate fluting, the fanciful enrichment of the mouldings, and the applied ornament in composition which the Adam brothers had first introduced, and which had become the fashion everywhere in France as well as in England.

Another characteristic feature of the work of the early Republic as against that of the Colonial day was its use of diverse forms of interior space—circular, elliptical, semi-circular—which vary the monotonous rectangularity of the rooms of the Colonial house.

Let us in our regional survey look first at the several types of mass of the houses as a whole, before we turn to matters of detail. For some time after the Revolution there was a survival of the Colonial forms without much fresh admixture, which we may speak of as post-Colonial work. One type which was characteristic of this moment is worthy to be signalized—the great three-story house adorned with pilasters at the corners as we see in the most famous example of it, the Peirce-Nichols house in Salem, erected actually during the closing years of the War. The three-story four-square house was already a familiar type in New England before the War, and the lower houses with pilasters were likewise common there then. The application of pilasters on such a grand scale to the three-story square house occurred, however, just at the close of the War, in a considerable number of houses in New England, generally to the north of Boston. It is a type readily recognizable, almost identical in certain examples, like the Peirce-Nichols house and the Kittredge house in North Andover, some twenty miles from Salem. In these houses, as in their distant descendant in Wiscasset here illustrated, one already finds the new spirit of classicism breathing faintly in their monumental dignity, although the forms as yet are simply those which had been current in the academic style before the War. There had not as yet appeared larger ideas of creative originality such as one finds about the year 1790 in all of the different colonies.

In New England, the protagonist of the new spirit was Bulfinch, and he created, I think we may say, all the principal novel types which became current throughout New England, types of plan as well as types of mass and surface treatment. For the plan, the favored model was his first domestic design, the Barrell house in Charlestown, in which he abandoned the tradition of a transverse stair-hall and introduced the scheme of a drawing-room or salon of elliptical form, occupying the place of honor in the center of the garden front opposite the entrance. This scheme, thoroughly French, had a number of merits, the chief perhaps being a subtle one, that of giving, as one progressed along the path of honor through the center, a variety of spatial effects, as the rooms and staircases opened to left and right with their varied terminations, rectangular, semi-circular and elliptical. This plan, which one might think of as highly exceptional, was employed in some dozen of the most notable houses of New England, and may be regarded as particularly characteristic of that section, although it was not confined to it. At New York, at Philadelphia, at Washington—in the most notable of all American houses, the White House—and at Charleston, there were isolated ambitious examples.

On the exterior, for surface treatment, we find the favorite formula of Bulfinch and his generation in New England to be that of tall pilasters above a high basement, perhaps with arcades, as in the Harrison Gray Otis house on Mt. Vernon Street, one of three magnificent houses built by this great social leader in Boston. The formula itself was not wholly novel—we can point to at least one example before the Revolution—but it was new as now used so frequently, with the elongation of the columns or pilasters, the delicacy of detail characteristic of the Adam style, and it became very typical of New England. For Elias Hasket Derby of Salem, the richest merchant of his time, Bulfinch designed a magnificent house on this general model. As modified by McIntire, Bulfinch's most faithful and gifted follower in the new style—which now came to him as a higher revelation—the design was executed in the marvellous, though short-lived and ill-fated mansion. Established by the work of these two men in numerous instances, the scheme was employed all over New England for some of the finest houses, such as the John or Daniel Pierce house at Portsmouth, or, still further north, the Churchill house in Portland, Maine. One might find it also in the Nathan Smith house in New Haven, and it thus represents a characteristically New England type, although one not without certain exemplars elsewhere.

No one who knows Boston could mistake the Prescott house on Beacon Street for one of any other city, because it belongs to another type established there by Bulfinch in some half dozen examples, and is part of the physiognomy of Beacon Hill—a house four stories in height with bow windows, extremely elongated pilasters, and the lower story fronted by the slenderest colonnettes, of which Bulfinch was specially fond.

Another type very justly associated with his name is the type of house with delicate blank arcadings. Two examples of which his actual authorship is not so certain are the Phelps house at Andover, and, distant from it in New England yet easily recognizable as related, the Wheeler house at Orford, New Hampshire. Far up the Connecticut River at the threshold of the White Mountains, it serves as an outpost of this Bostonian style for which Bulfinch was ultimately responsible.

It was Bulfinch also, with his preoccupation with varied forms of mass and space, who introduced in New England a feature used soon afterwards at Charleston and in the White House at Washington—the semi-circular portico. It was inaugurated on a grand scale in the Barrell house, and was immediately imitated by McIntire and others in the small semi-circular door porticos, which are characteristic of Salem after 1793.

It was primarily in Massachusetts and Virginia, the states which furnished the first six Presidents, that the new style took its rise. The Massachusetts seacoast towns were perhaps the first to profit by the Revolution, but the great Virginia plantations—at least in the Piedmont—had also, for a moment, a new bloom following the War. The counterpart of Derby as the first millionaire of the North, was Washington, not only the most distinguished but the richest planter of the South, whose wealth at his death reached about the same figure. Like the English gentleman of the time, and the Virginia gentleman also, Washington took an active interest in architecture, and no doubt was personally responsible for the ideas as well as for drawing the forms in the remodelling of Mt. Vernon at the close of the War. It was then that the enlarged house was fronted by the long portico with which we are so familiar, rising through the full height of the house. Square piers, employed perhaps because of lack of technical means for turning circular columns, were given a vogue, as we shall see, by this very conspicuous instance of their use.

It was, however, less Washington, representing the dying generation of the Tidewater planters whose prosperity was soon to vanish, than Jefferson, representative of the new men of the Piedmont, who established what became the characteristic Southern type. This is the house with the temple portico, crowned by the triangular classical pediment, as we see it most notably in his own house at Monticello. In many respects, such as its dome, this house surpassed all the others in its classical extremes. The porticos which adorned both sides of the house are what became typical of the great Southern Piedmont plantation houses all up and down the Blue Ridge from the Potomac into Georgia.

In speaking of characteristic local types, we should not pass over one of very extraordinary character—confined to Richmond and likewise traceable to Jefferson—the house with two bay windows, filled in between with an arcade, of which there were formerly many examples there; and even today, after all the vicissitudes of fire, a notable one still stands.

In the populous regions between these two great colonies we find other local characteristics, partly traceable indeed to special persons. In Maryland, William Thornton, whose design for the Capitol in Washington had received the first prize, exercised a substantial influence through a design I firmly believe to be his, although the conviction does not rest on any document—that for Homewood, now absorbed in the city of Baltimore and the grounds of Johns Hopkins University. Thornton's style was a delicate version of the Adam, and the portico as he employed it was slender and of a delicacy not found in the monumental work under Jefferson's inspiration.

With Philadelphia everyone associates the combination of red brick and white or gray marble, there a local material. Among the houses of Germantown, Wyck, the most beautiful of all, assumed the form in which we now see it at the hands of a late apostle of the Greek revival, William Strickland, whose name was formerly synonymous for all that was pedantic in that archæological version of American classic style. It was he who remodelled the house in 1826. We must grant him the distinction of having known when to discriminate between the monumental and the domestic.

Contrary to popular opinion, by far the greater number of the houses about New York, with eastern New Jersey and Long Island, came from the time after the piazza was popularized as a feature of these houses. Just on the eve of the War we find the painter Copley describing this to his brother in Boston, to whom it was wholly unknown. The Hewlett house at Woodbury on Long Island is a simple example of what one may call the vernacular version. The finer examples were influenced, in spite of the great distance, by Mt. Vernon. Who can deny the close analogy between Mt. Vernon and such an example of the style at its finest in the Vreeland house at Nordhoff, New Jersey, with its very tall square pillars rising to the main cornice? The mediating agent is easily found in the widespread distribution of engravings of the home of the father of his country. The gambrel roof persisted notably in these Dutch houses, long after the War, in spite of the fact that as a type it did not belong to the new order of thought. A multitude of picturesque examples, such as the Dyckman house on Manhattan, testify to its popularity after the Revolution. In the great majority of houses the roof rises from eaves only one story up, and this remains true even where there is an ordinary pitch roof. On Long Island one sees the persistence also of those materials, such as the long shingle, which are characteristic of the Dutch Colonial style.

When we turn from the general types of houses to study the forms of detail, we encounter two persistent fallacies. One of them, the product of ignorance of European developments, now happily dying, attributed the attenuation of the post-Revolutionary work to naïve adaptation of classical forms, originally developed in stone, to a material, wood, which was thought of as characteristically American. The view overlooked the widespread use of wood in England at the same time, and the fact that the attenuation was the fruit of a purely formal development of style, the influence of Pompeian suggestion on the Adams and their following.

The other fallacy, still flourishing, is the idea that many characteristic details were derived by the American craftsmen from the furniture books. It arises chiefly from the fact that Chippendale's great book of furniture designs is far more familiar to us today than the many builders' handbooks of the same period. All these details are to be found in them, often earlier than in Chippendale, and sometimes where he does not show them at all.

Most of the features that have been regarded as of American origin are to be found in English architectural books. Perhaps the most characteristic is the "fret dentil bedmould"—cut at the top to form part of a continuous fretted band. This is shown in Abraham Swan's *Designs in Architecture* in 1757, of which a Philadelphia edition appeared in 1775, and in the third edition of William Pain's *Builder's Companion* in 1769. A variant, the "eye dentil," with auger holes at the foot of each cut, much used in America, appears in Pain's *British Palladio*, 1786. The use of guttæ as dentils occurs here first, so far as we know, in the cornice of the William Grey house, Salem, 1801. It is shown by Pain in 1786. What may be called "Gothic dentils," a series of small groined arches resting on tiny corbels, which occur, for instance, in the Miles Brewton house, Charleston, 1765–69, and in the John Pierce house, Portsmouth, about 1800, are shown in Pain's *Builder's Companion*, 1758. We are thus guarded from over-estimating the novelty of the American work which contains these features.

We would be doing the American carpenter less than justice, however, if we did not recognize that, while the suggestion for these adaptations of classical elements to his ordinary tools had, like so many other features, their origins in England, he gave them an extreme and very imaginative development. A half dozen examples will suffice: the leaf-like forms filled with auger holes, as shown in the *American Builder's Companion* of Asher Benjamin in 1806, and found in numerous examples, especially in the Connecticut Valley where he did his first actual work; the use of the gouge and auger in adaptations of Adam fluting; and the suggestion of garlands by devices of elementary simplicity. The sunbursts which form such a characteristic feature of the Adam style were likewise given a modified form by the local carpenter, as in many examples here illustrated.

Such features in general know no local habitat, but in certain regions there is a special concentration of them. Thus for instance at Providence and Bristol there is a great elaboration of the Chinese lattice-work, already popular before the Revolution, which took on in this region an unequalled development. One sees it in the Paddleford house at Providence

in the rails of porch and eaves, and in the Churchill house at Bristol, where it especially flourished. In the Morris house at Bristol, almost the sole decorative motive is the multiplication of its lattices.

The doorway, after the Revolution, found its characteristic form in the type with side-lights and some sort of transom. Any door in America which has side-lights comes from after the Revolution. Side-lights and fanlights are found everywhere, the fanlight usually in elliptical form. Just the nuance of detail that we see in the doorways added by Madame Jumel to the Roger Morris house in New York, and in that of the Vreeland house at Nordhoff —the great multiplication of breaks, the curved fragments of cornice—could be found only around New York, and in its western hinterland, several times exemplified in this book. A form of early Republican doorway, with a horizontal transom instead of an elliptical one, later became particularly associated with New York and its sphere of influence, as in the example at Rodman's Neck. By that time this sphere was very great, extending as it did along the great western waterway formed by the Hudson, the Erie Canal, and the Lakes, to the further shores of Lake Michigan.

When we come to the interior of the house, we find ourselves in the chief field for the flowering of the Adam ornament. Its most notable feature was the chimney-piece. In what we may call the standard Republican form, the fireplace is flanked by some type of columnar element. Several variants occur: the single panelled pilaster, and the pair of colonnettes, might be found anywhere in America. We must not exaggerate the local character of such forms until we have made sure by wide search that they do not recur at widely isolated points, as is true in most cases. Thus, for instance, one mantel from a Lancaster house, which has colonnettes in Gothic form, is duplicated line for line in a mantel from the William Grey house in Salem. Similarly the employment of baluster-like forms as the supports, which has been thought to be a feature particularly characteristic of the region around New York, of the "Dutch Colonial," recurs in our Lancaster house. One perceives that all these varied manners of treatment existed side by side in the same locality.

Truly special types are only found in a few localities. One of those is Portsmouth and its sphere of influence, including the Merrimac Valley. The chimney-piece of the Haven house at Portsmouth has very slender colonnettes, not only flanking the fireplace but also the over-mantel. The same scheme is found in the mantel from the Eagle house at Haverhill, in the Metropolitan Museum.

We have been speaking thus far of the general types of the chimney-piece, but we must not fail to discuss its most conspicuous feature, the ornaments. They took their suggestion from the composition ornaments which had been developed by the Adam brothers. There can be no doubt that the ornaments of the great majority of the earlier American examples were imported. Exactly the same pair of end ornaments is found on an English mantel in Hatton Garden, London, and in what is no doubt one of the oldest of such chimney-pieces now left in New England, in the Harrison Grey Otis house in Boston. From their very date, coupled with this identity, we realize that these ornaments must have been casts from the English moulds. Most of the ornaments were imported even for the chimney-pieces of a designer like Samuel McIntire, who was also a skilled carver in wood. Not to him, in these instances, but to the maker of the moulds, are to be attributed the delicacy and beauty of the ornaments. The differences in the work of the different men lay rather in the selection and disposition of the ornaments, in which we can often trace a personal note. McIntire, moreover, did carve a number of his ornaments, instead of employing composition. That was particularly true where they were patriotic motives, much in vogue in the time of the Embargo and later. A typical instance of one of McIntire's eagle ornaments appears in the mantel of the Registry of Deeds in Salem, built in 1807. At times also, stimu-lated perhaps by the difficulty of securing importations, due to the Embargo, he carved other ornaments, such as the beautiful festoons with fruit on the mantel from the Lindall-Barnard-Andrews house at Salem.

The same cause encouraged the employment of American-made composition ornaments. Robert Welford of Philadelphia claimed the honor of being the first American manufacturer of these. His name appears on the sarcophagus "To the memory of departed heroes" in a mantel from Pennsylvania in one of the rooms of the American Wing of the Metropolitan Museum. No doubt it was he also who made the central ornament of the other mantel in the same room, which shows Perry's victory at Lake Erie. The patriotic emblems, so far as we know, were from American makers. The more familiar classical emblems continued to be imported, but doubtless in the course of his work Welford reproduced also certain of these favorite English motives. Some of the American examples of consecrated types seem to have been produced from moulds carved from the imported ornaments.

While in some of these instances the supposed originality of our craftsmen does not gain, in others we have to admire their ingenuity and creative ability. Among those are especially the ones in which, whether from lack of means, difficulty of importation in troubled times, or from preference, the familiar ideas of the Adam cycle were translated into the product of the ordinary tools of the carver—the gouge and auger. Many rich examples come from the sphere of Philadelphia where this type of work was much used, so much so as to call down the condemnation of Owen Biddle, a Philadelphia writer on architecture of that day: "In ornamenting a mantel, the young carpenter would do well to endeavor at an imitation of something natural, and not to cover his work with unmeaning holes and cuttings of a gouge."* Today we justly recognize the value of these as pure designs, and the very charming ap-

*The Young Carpenter's Assistant (1817), p. 28. The first edition appeared in 1805. This passage was kindly called to my attention by Lawrence Kocher.

proximation to the Adam garlands and rosettes by simple means.

It would be a mistake to suppose that this type of work was limited only to Philadelphia, or even its surrounding towns, like Newcastle. Many mantels elsewhere are full of it, for instance one in the Haven house in Portsmouth. So, too, it would be a mistake to suppose that the fan or sunburst, so commonly found around New York work, was wholly confined to that locality. We find an example in Old Lyme, Connecticut, and one almost identical with it in Carlisle, Pennsylvania. A more characteristically local form, with multiplied reedings of extreme delicacy, occurs in Baltimore and is conspicuously exemplified in the room from Baltimore in the American Wing of the Metropolitan Museum. Almost the sole adornments are the multiplied reed-ings, sometimes swelling in oval pilasters and sometimes dipping into niches.

We do right not to echo the contemporary condemnations of Biddle against such manifestations of style but to value them as products of native American craftsmanship.

We see in the work of the early Republic how vastly widened had been the scope of design, how many localities, now first achieving their prosperity, created their own local traditions and characteristic styles. So strong are these as even to have paralyzed new artistic creation. One can scarcely build on Beacon Hill, it has seemed, except in the style of Bulfinch; in the Piedmont, except in the style of Jefferson; or in Baltimore, except in the style of Thornton, Latrobe, and Mills.

Fiske Kimball

The South Façade

THE SHADOWS, ON THE BAYOU TECHE, NEW IBERIA, LOUISIANA

THE SOUTH FAÇADE

THE SHADOWS, ON THE BAYOU TECHE, NEW IBERIA, LOUISIANA

24

THE SOUTH PORCH

THE SHADOWS, ON THE BAYOU TECHE, NEW IBERIA, LOUISIANA

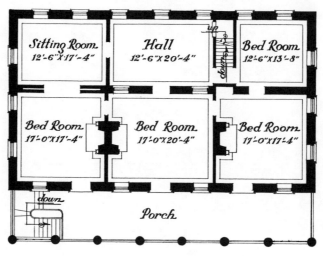

Sitting Room.
12'-6"x17'-4"

Hall
12'-6"x20'-4"

up

Bed Room.
12'-6"x13'-8"

Bed Room.
17'-0"x17'-4"

Bed Room.
17'-0"x20'-4"

Bed Room.
17'-0"x17'-4"

down

Porch.

Second Floor Plan

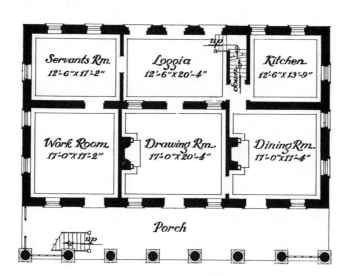

up

Servants Rm.
12'-6"x17'-2"

Loggia
12'-6"x20'-4"

down

Kitchen.
12'-6"x13'-9"

Work Room.
17'-0"x17'-2"

Drawing Rm.
17'-0"x20'-4"

Dining Rm.
17'-0"x17'-4"

Porch.

up

First Floor Plan

"THE SHADOWS"   THE OLD WEEKS HOUSE
New Iberia, Louisiana
Built in 1830 · Now Owned by W. W. Hall Esq.

graphic 0' 5' 10' 15' 20' scale

South Elevation
· Watercolor by A. PERSAC ~ 1861 ·

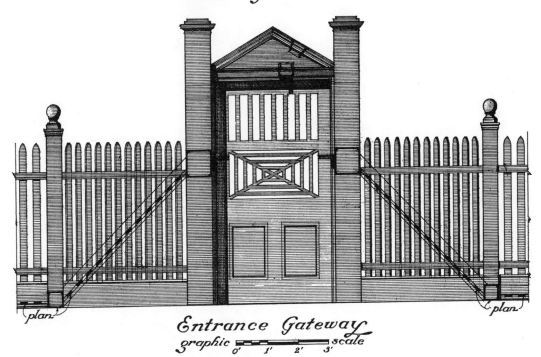

plan   *plan*

Entrance Gateway
graphic ▭▭▭▭▭ scale
0'   1'   2'   3'

"THE SHADOWS" THE OLD WEEKS HOUSE
New Iberia, Louisiana
Built in 1830 · Now Owned by W. W. Hall Esq.

WATERCOLOR BY A. PERSAC, 1861

THE SHADOWS, ON THE BAYOU TECHE, NEW IBERIA, LOUISIANA

Photograph by Martin's Studio

THE NORTH FAÇADE

THE SHADOWS, ON THE BAYOU TECHE, NEW IBERIA, LOUISIANA

The Entrance Façade

ROSEDOWN, NEAR ST. FRANCISVILLE, LOUISIANA

Rosedown was the model for
Portobello, the Bedford's house,
in *So Red the Rose*
                    Stark Young
December 9, 1936.

Rosedown

The Bowman Plantation, St. Francisville, Louisiana.

Built by Daniel Turnbull in 1835.

Graphic Scale

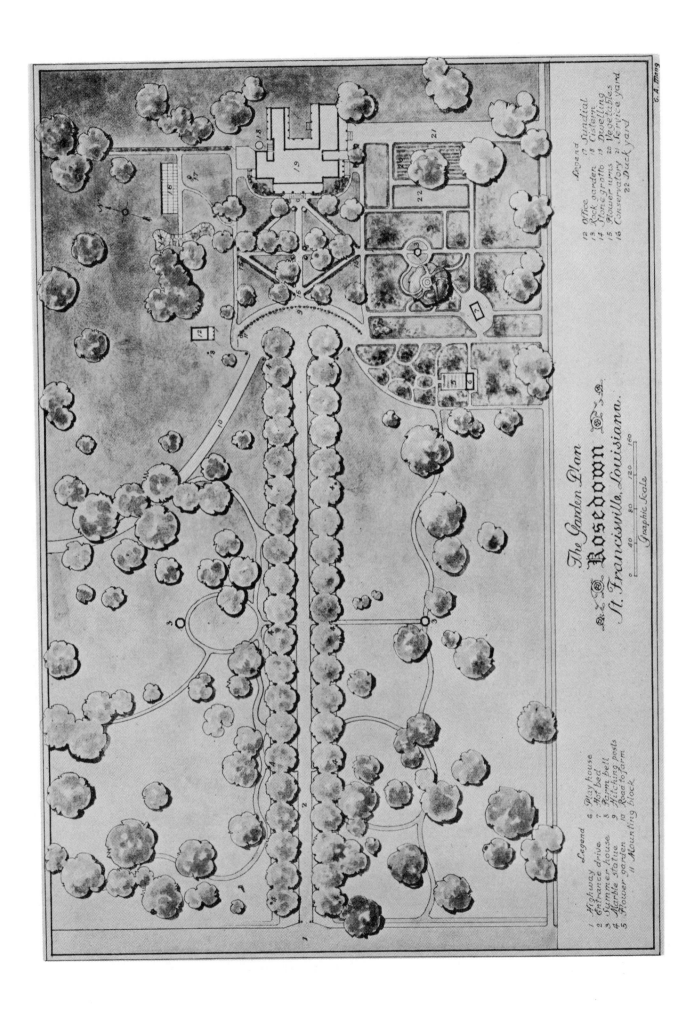

The Garden Plan
Rosedown
St. Francisville, Louisiana.

Graphic Scale

G. A. Tung

Drive Through the Grounds

Photographs by Memphis Photographic Co.

The Office

ROSEDOWN, NEAR ST. FRANCISVILLE, LOUISIANA

Statues Lining the Oak Alley

The Turn-around before the House — Looking down the oak alley and showing the
vases and the statues of Europe, Asia, Africa and America brought from France

ROSEDOWN, NEAR ST. FRANCISVILLE, LOUISIANA

33

Photograph by Memphis Photographic Co.

THE GARDEN PAVILION, CIRCA 1828 — PAINTED A PALE BLUE GREY, PROBABLY BY
FRENCH WORKMEN FROM NEW ORLEANS (INDICATED 3 ON GARDEN PLAN)

ROSEDOWN, NEAR ST. FRANCISVILLE, LOUISIANA

North Elevation

·D'EVEREUX·

1/16" 1 Foot

Scale

NATCHEZ · ADAMS COUNTY · MISSISSIPPI · USA ·

L. P. Rixford del.

D'EVEREUX, NEAR NATCHEZ, ADAMS COUNTY, MISSISSIPPI

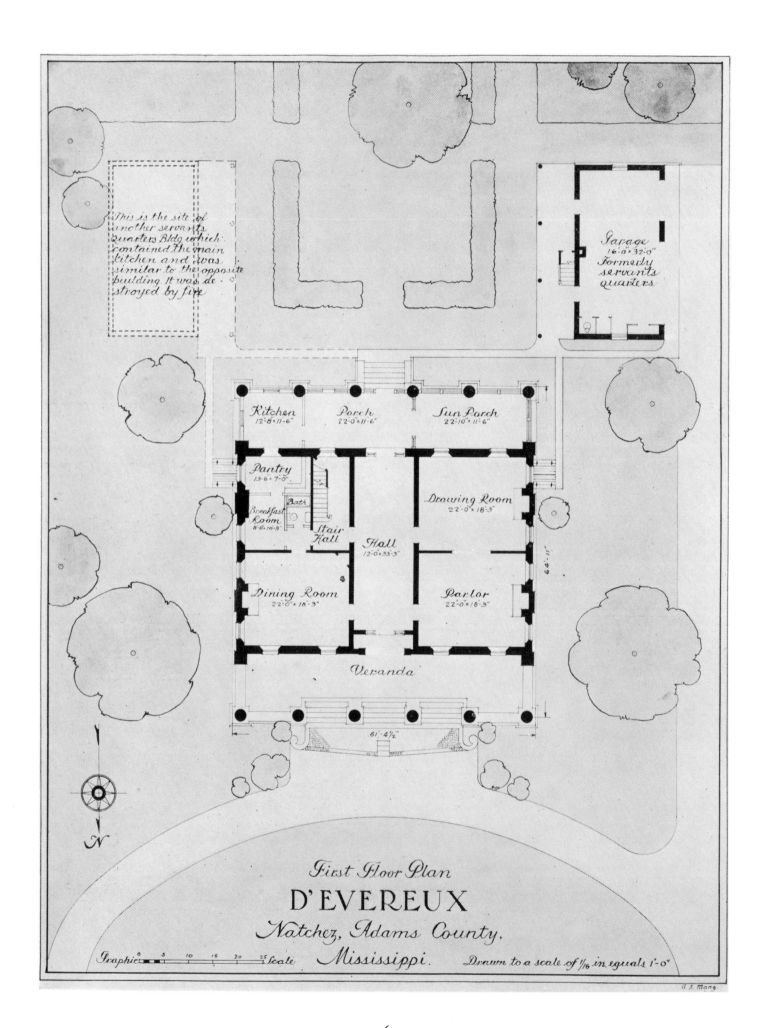

This is the site of another servants Quarters Bldg which contained the main kitchen and was similar to the opposite building. It was destroyed by fire

Garage
16'-0"x32'-0"
Formerly servants quarters

Kitchen
12'-8"x11'-6"

Porch
22'-0"x11'-6"

Sun Porch
22'-10"x11'-6"

Pantry
13'-6"x7'-0"

Drawing Room
22'-0"x18'-3"

Bath

Breakfast Room
8'-0"x10'-9"

Stair Hall

Hall
12'-0"x33'-3"

64'-11"

Dining Room
22'-0"x18'-3"

Parlor
22'-0"x18'-3"

Veranda

61'-4½"

N

First Floor Plan
D'EVEREUX
Natchez, Adams County.
Mississippi.

Graphic 0 5 10 15 20 25 Scale   Drawn to a scale of 1/16 in. equals 1'-0"

Two Views from the North

D'EVEREUX, NEAR NATCHEZ, ADAMS COUNTY, MISSISSIPPI

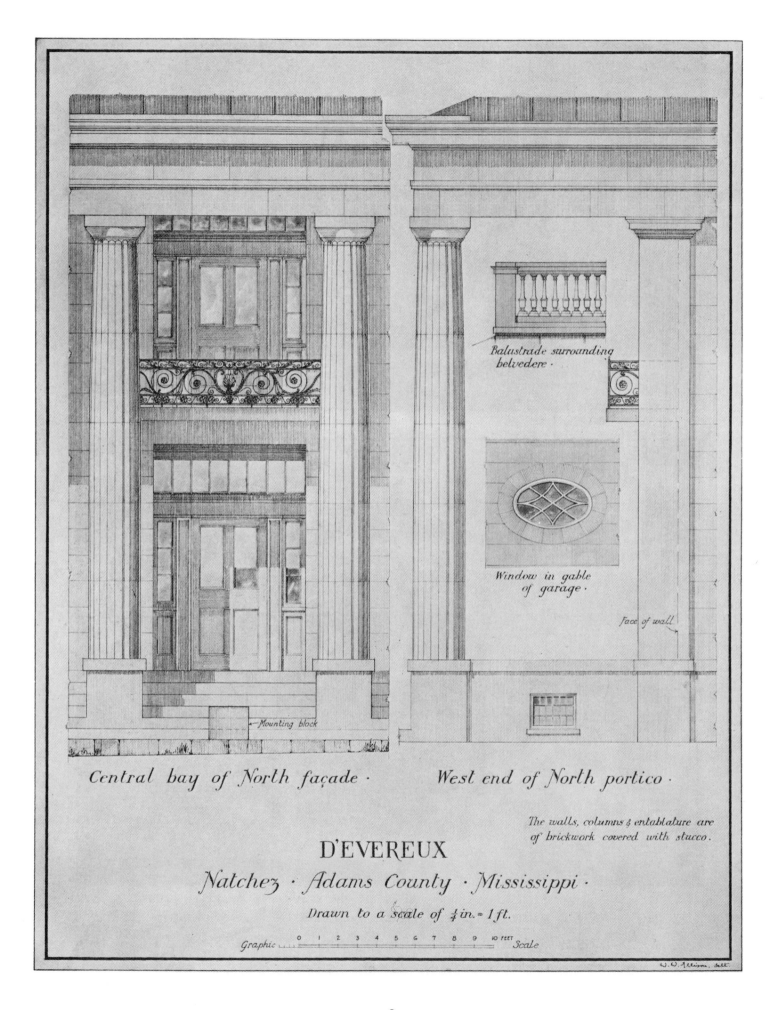

Central bay of North façade ·

West end of North portico ·

Balustrade surrounding belvedere ·

Window in gable of garage ·

Face of wall

Mounting block

The walls, columns & entablature are of brickwork covered with stucco.

D'EVEREUX
Natchez · Adams County · Mississippi ·
Drawn to a scale of ¼ in. = 1 ft.

Graphic   0 1 2 3 4 5 6 7 8 9   10 FEET   Scale

VIEW FROM THE NORTH

GLOUCESTER, NATCHEZ, ADAMS COUNTY, MISSISSIPPI

NORTH — ELEVATION OF GLOUCESTER

NATCHEZ, ADAMS CO., MISSISSIPPI

GRAPHIC SCALE

SCALE : 1 INCH = 12 FEET

K. DE GROOTE

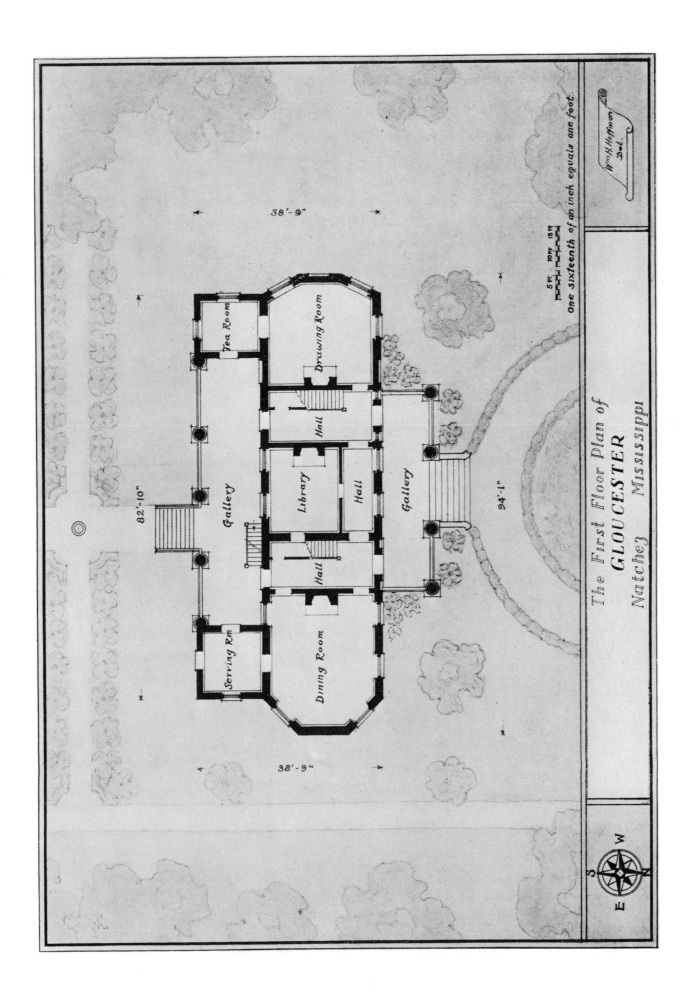

The First Floor Plan of
GLOUCESTER
Natchez   Mississippi

One sixteenth of an inch equals one foot.

Wm H Hoffman
Del.

THE SOUTH ELEVATION

THE FIRST-FLOOR NORTH HALL

GLOUCESTER, NATCHEZ, ADAMS COUNTY, MISSISSIPPI

Photograph by James Ross Gillie

VIEW FROM THE EAST

BELLE ISLE, NEAR GEORGETOWN, SOUTH CAROLINA

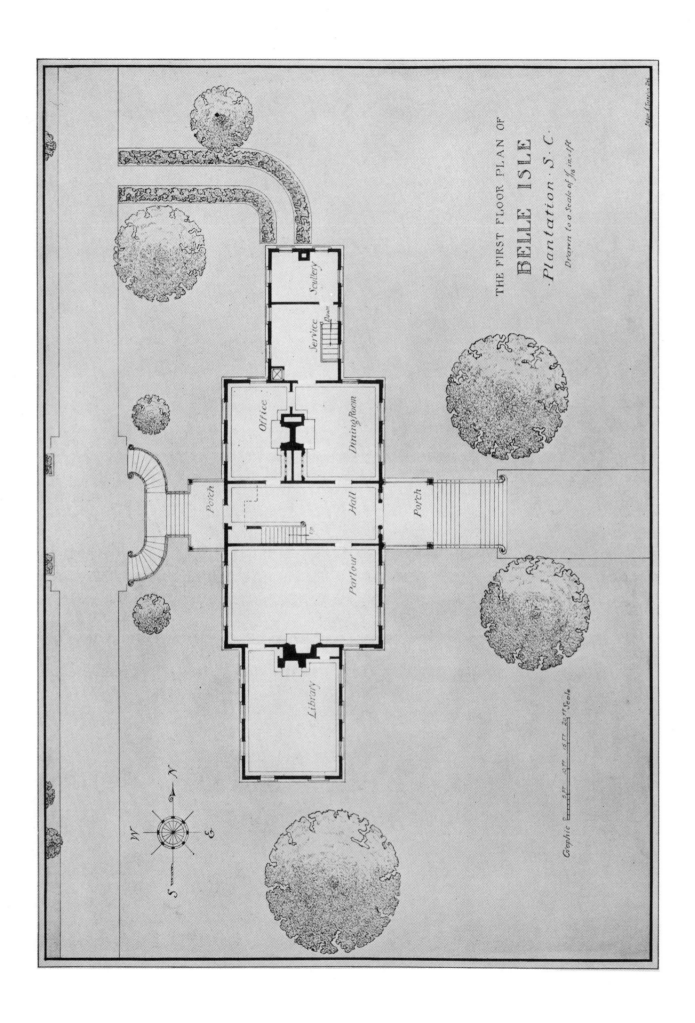

THE FIRST FLOOR PLAN OF

BELLE ISLE

Plantation · S · C ·

Drawn to a Scale of 1/16 in. 1ft

Scullery

Service

Office

Dining Room

Porch

Hall

Porch

Parlour

Library

Graphic Scale

Belle Isle
Plantation at Georgetown
South Carolina

Graphic Scale

· Detail of East Porch ·

Pediment
cornice

Main
cornice

· BELLE ISLE ·

Plantation, S·C·

Drawn to a scale of ⅛ in. = 1 ft.

Profiles are drawn
to a scale of
1 Inch = 1 foot .

Graphic   1   2   3   4   5   6 FEET   Scale

W.W.Ellison delt.

46

CARVED WOOD
CENTERPIECE ON
THE DRAWING-ROOM
CEILING

Photographs by
James Ross Gillie

THE ENTRANCE PORCH

DETAIL OF THE ENTRANCE PORTICO

BELLE ISLE, NEAR GEORGETOWN, SOUTH CAROLINA

47

DETAIL OF THE MAIN STAIRCASE

DETAIL OF THE PARLOR
WALLPAPER, PRINTED IN
TEMPERA IN FULL COLOR

Photographs by James Ross Gillie

BELLE ISLE, NEAR GEORGETOWN, SOUTH CAROLINA

View from the Southwest

MULBERRY CASTLE, ON THE COOPER RIVER, SOUTH CAROLINA

Mulberry Castle
Cooper River – South Carolina
Built Between 1708 & 1725
Graphic Scale

M.W. Bacon Jr.

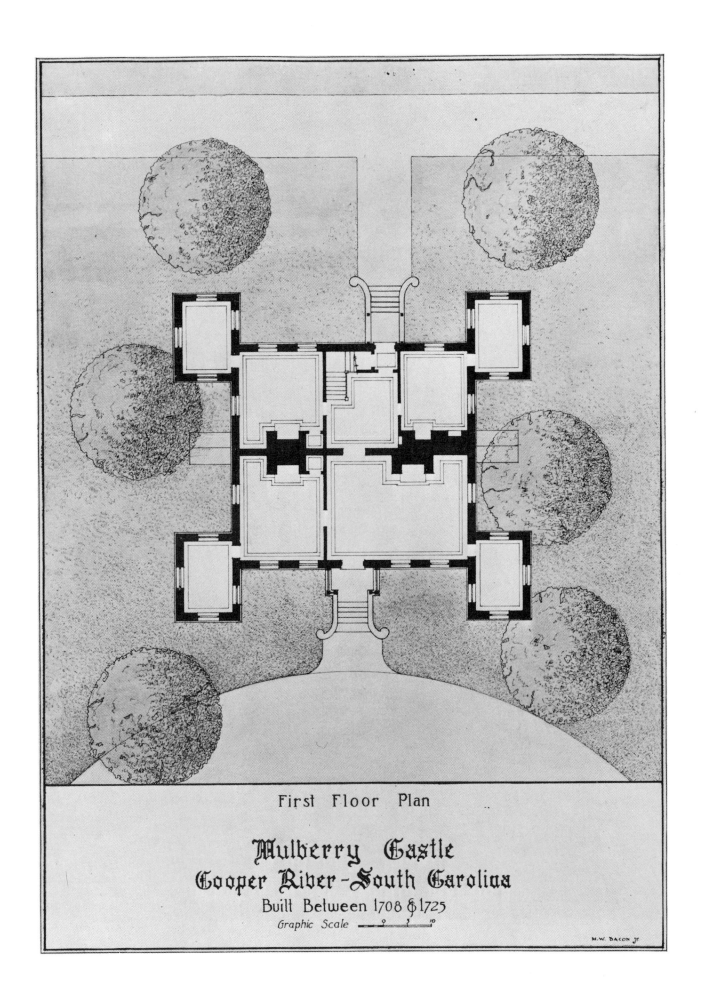

First Floor Plan

Mulberry Castle
Cooper River—South Carolina
Built Between 1708 & 1725

Graphic Scale

M.W. Bacon Jr

Photograph by James Ross Gillie

DETAIL OF THE NORTHWEST TOWER

MULBERRY CASTLE, ON THE COOPER RIVER, SOUTH CAROLINA

Photographs by James Ross Gillie

A First-floor Door Jamb

A Door in the Second-floor Hall

Detail of an Interior Door

MULBERRY CASTLE, ON THE COOPER RIVER, SOUTH CAROLINA

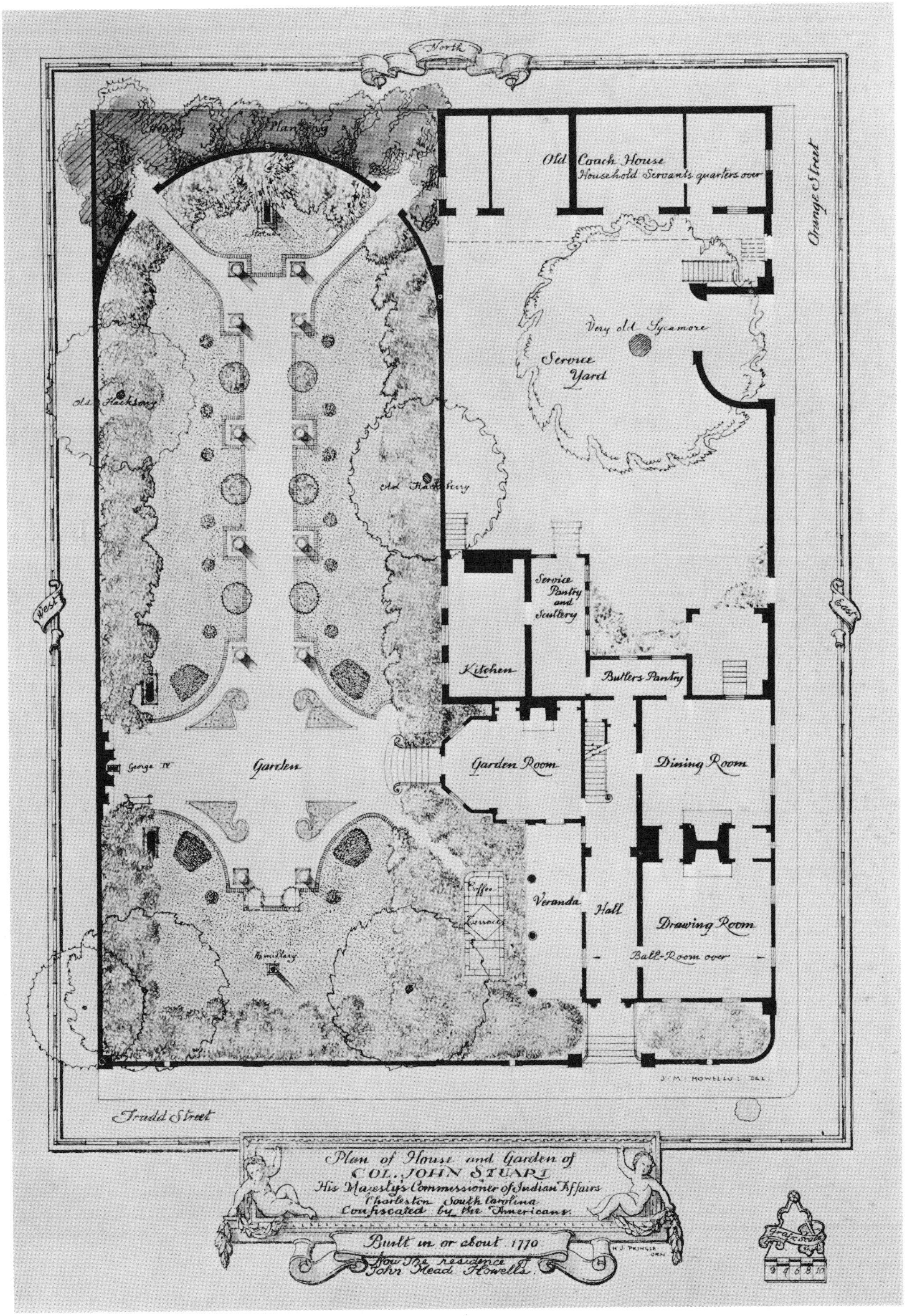
North
Old Coach House
Household Servants quarters over
Orange Street
Very old Sycamore
Service Yard
Old Hackberry
Service Pantry and Scullery
Kitchen
Butlers Pantry
Garden Room
Dining Room
Garden
Veranda
Hall
Drawing Room
Ball-Room over
West
East
Tradd Street
J. M. HOWELLS: DEL.
Plan of House and Garden of
COL. JOHN STUART
His Majesty's Commissioner of Indian Affairs
Charleston South Carolina
Confiscated by the Americans
Built in or about 1770
Now the residence of
John Mead Howells

THE COLONEL JOHN STUART HOUSE, CHARLESTON, SOUTH CAROLINA

Key Block

A·A

C·C

D·D

B·B

One half Bracket

E·E

G·G

F·F

Detail of the Entrance Doorway & Window
of
The Col. John Stuart House
Charleston South Carolina
Circa 1770

Scale of Elevation
0 1 2 3 4 feet

Scale of Details
6 inches   one foot

H. J. Pringle - del.

THE ENTRANCE

THE COLONEL JOHN STUART HOUSE, CHARLESTON, SOUTH CAROLINA

Now owned by Mr. John Mead Howells

THE BALL ROOM

THE COLONEL JOHN STUART HOUSE, CHARLESTON, SOUTH CAROLINA

The Drawing Room

Photographs by Samuel H. Gottscho

The Quarters at the Rear of the Garden

THE COLONEL JOHN STUART HOUSE, CHARLESTON, SOUTH CAROLINA

SOUTH FAÇADE

Stuart Mansion. Charleston. South Carolina. Built in or about 1770
by COL. JOHN STUART. His Majesty's Commissioner of Indian
Affairs, Member of Council in Virginia, the Carolinas, Georgia
and Florida. The House was confiscated by the Americans.

Grafic Scale ▭▭▭▭ 5 ▭▭ 10 ft.   Actual Scale ⅛ inch=one foot

H. L. Pringle del.

THE ENTRANCE PORTICO AS SEEN TODAY

SABINE HALL, RICHMOND COUNTY, VIRGINIA

The North East or
Sabine Hall - Rich
Built by Land
Drawn to the scal

...eway Facade of
...d County-Virginia
...arter in 1730
... feet equal 1 inch ——

Louis Di Carlo R.T.

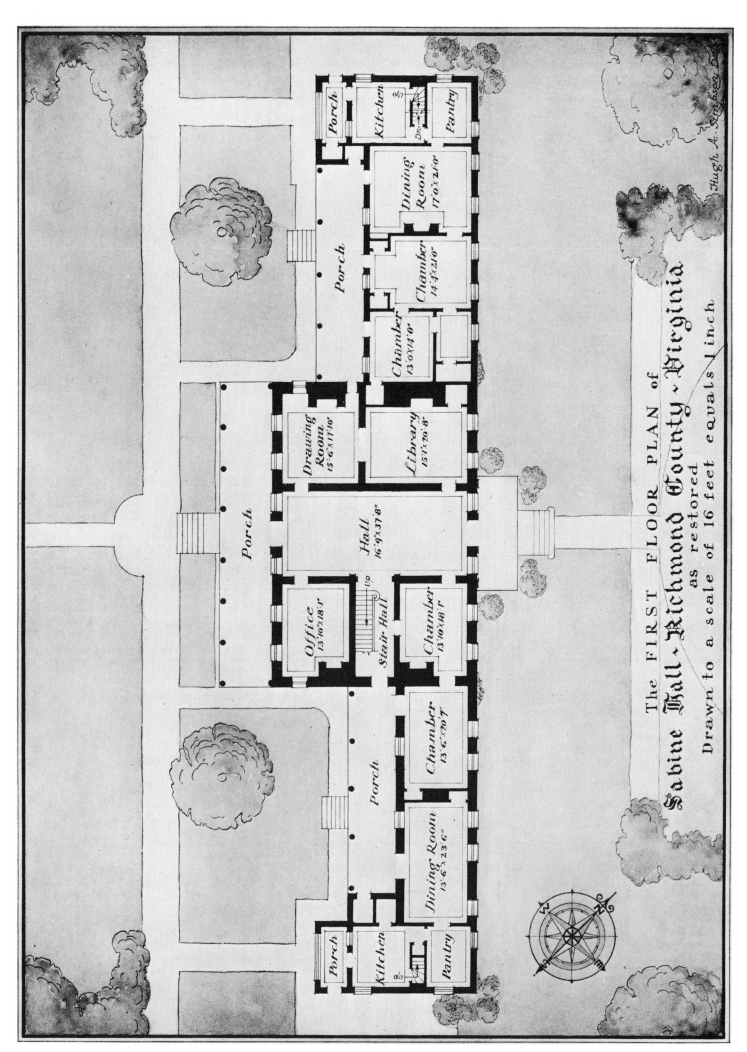

The FIRST FLOOR PLAN of
Sabine Hall ~ Richmond County ~ Virginia
as restored
Drawn to a scale of 16 feet equals 1 inch

Hugh A. Forbes Del.

Photographs by James Ross Gillie

DETAIL OF THE ENTRANCE PORTICO

SABINE HALL, RICHMOND COUNTY, VIRGINIA

SERVICE WING AND CELLAR STAIRWAY AT THE EAST END

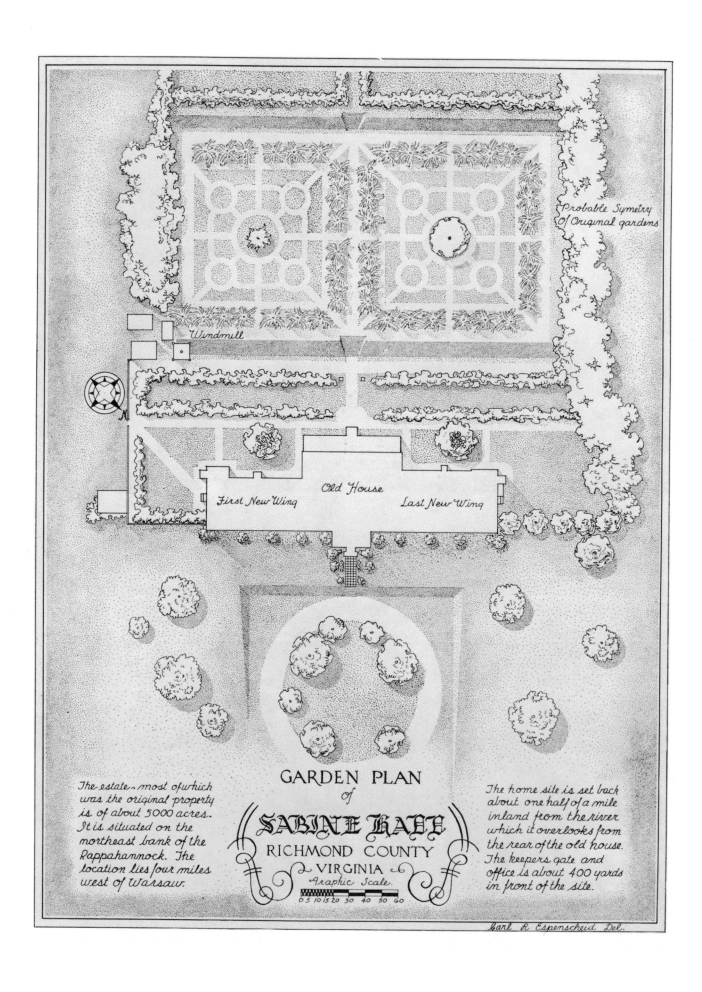

Probable Symetry
of Original gardens

Windmill

Old House

First New Wing   Last New Wing

GARDEN PLAN
of
SABINE HALL
RICHMOND COUNTY
VIRGINIA
Graphic Scale.
0 5 10 15 20 30 40 50 60

The estate, most of which was the original property is of about 5000 acres. It is situated on the northeast bank of the Rappahannock. The location lies four miles west of Warsaw.

The home site is set back about one half of a mile inland from the river which it overlooks from the rear of the old house. The keepers gate and office is about 400 yards in front of the site.

Carl R Espenscheid Del.

GENERAL VIEW FROM THE SOUTH

TUCKAHOE, GOOCHLAND COUNTY, VIRGINIA

The North or Entrance Façade of

Tuckahoe ~ Goochland County ~ Virginia

Built by THOMAS RANDOLF About 1690

Graphic Scale.

Louis Keefoed. Del.

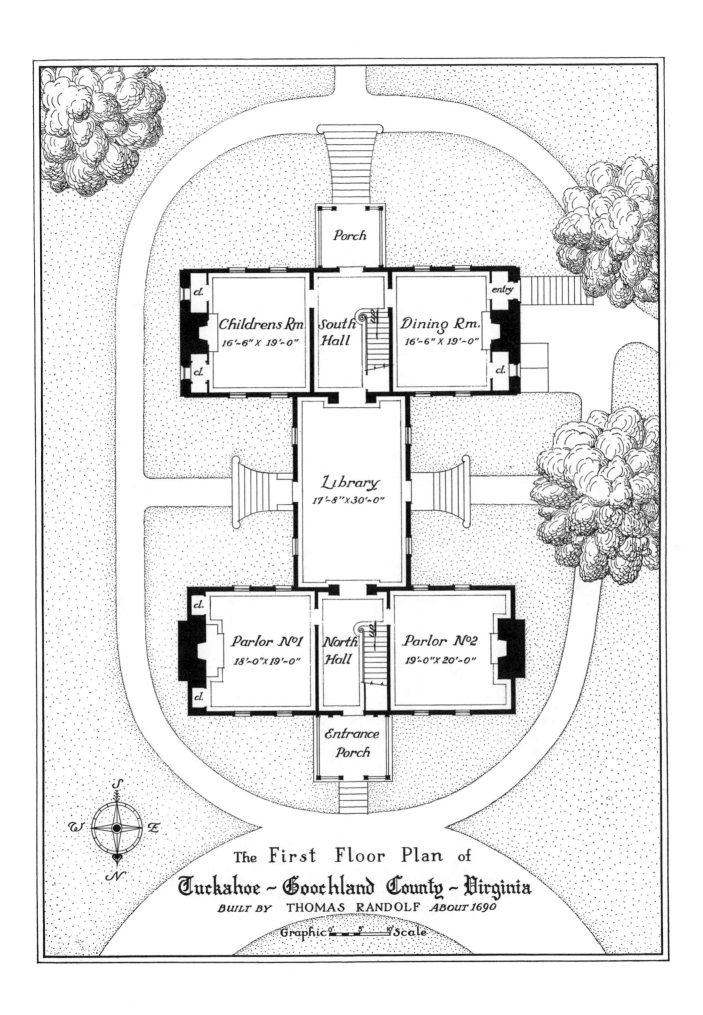

Porch

cl. | Childrens Rm | South | Dining Rm. | entry
16'-6" X 19'-0" | Hall | 16'-6" X 19'-0"
cl. | | | | cl.

Library
17'-8" X 30'-0"

cl. | Parlor Nº1 | North | Parlor Nº2
18'-0" X 19'-0" | Hall | 19'-0" X 20'-0"
cl.

Entrance
Porch

The First Floor Plan of
Tuckahoe ~ Goochland County ~ Virginia
BUILT BY THOMAS RANDOLF ABOUT 1690
Graphic 0 __ 5 __ 10' Scale

DETAIL OF THE SOUTH PORCH

TUCKAHOE, GOOCHLAND COUNTY, VIRGINIA

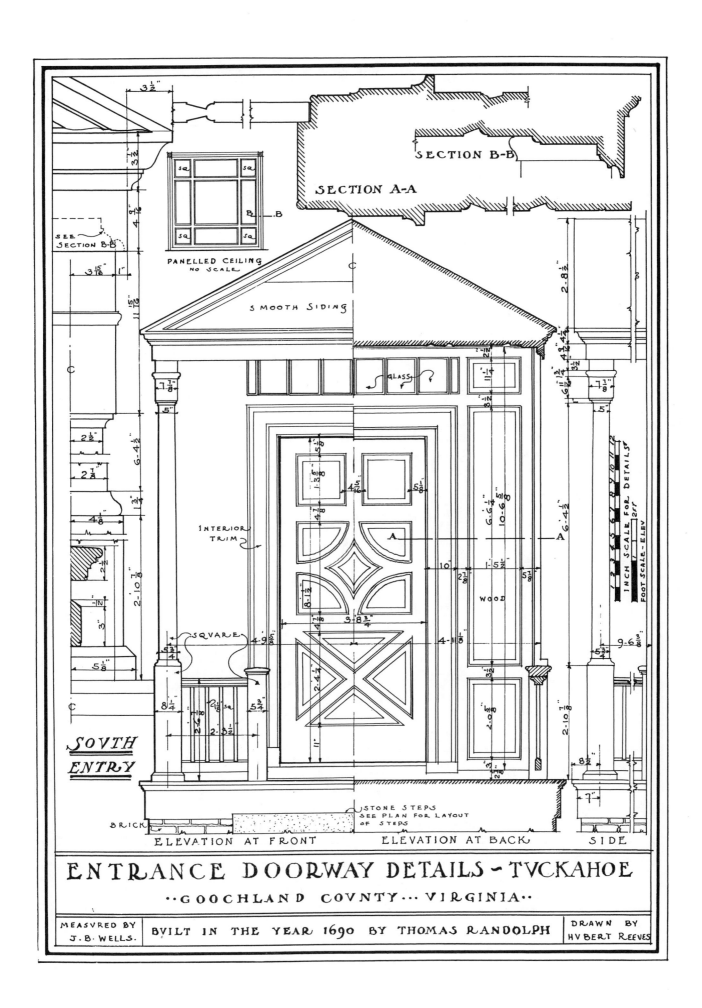

SECTION B-B

SECTION A-A

PANELLED CEILING
NO SCALE

SMOOTH SIDING

GLASS

SEE
SECTION B-B

INTERIOR
TRIM

SQVARE

WOOD

INCH SCALE FOR DETAILS

FOOT SCALE - ELEV

SOVTH
ENTRY

STONE STEPS
SEE PLAN FOR LAYOUT
OF STEPS

BRICK

ELEVATION AT FRONT

ELEVATION AT BACK

SIDE

ENTRANCE DOORWAY DETAILS - TVCKAHOE

··GOOCHLAND COVNTY··· VIRGINIA··

MEASVRED BY
J.B.WELLS.

BVILT IN THE YEAR 1690 BY THOMAS RANDOLPH

DRAWN BY
HVBERT REEVES

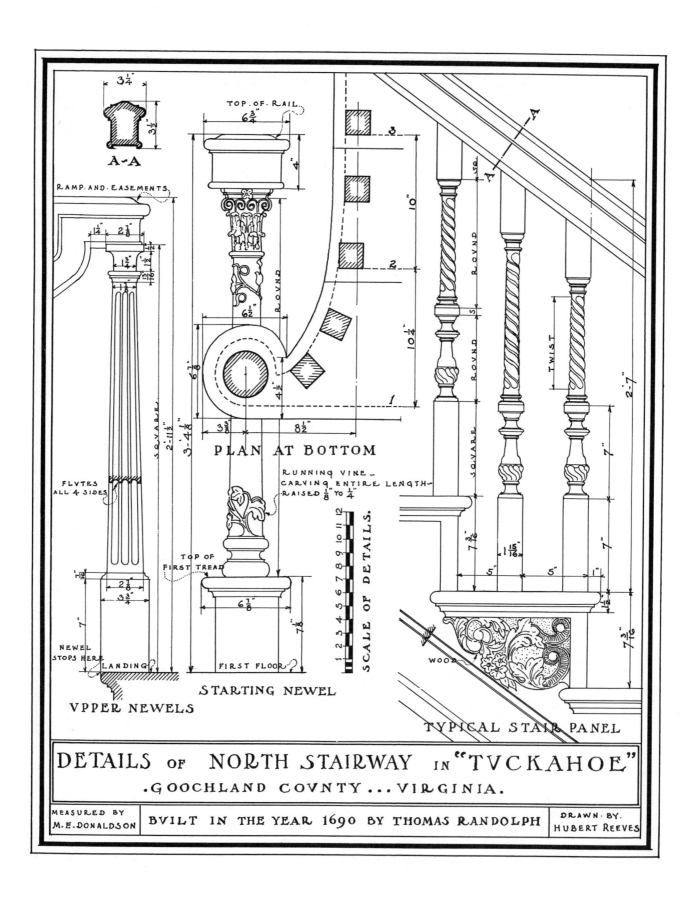

A-A

RAMP·AND·EASEMENTS

TOP·OF·RAIL

PLAN AT BOTTOM

RUNNING VINE―
CARVING ENTIRE LENGTH―
RAISED ⅛" TO ¼"

FLVTES
ALL 4 SIDES

TOP OF
FIRST TREAD

SCALE OF DETAILS.

NEWEL
STOPS HERE

LANDING

FIRST FLOOR

STARTING NEWEL

VPPER NEWELS

WOOD

TYPICAL STAIR PANEL

DETAILS of NORTH STAIRWAY in "TVCKAHOE"

·GOOCHLAND COVNTY ... VIRGINIA.

MEASURED BY
M.E.DONALDSON | BVILT IN THE YEAR 1690 BY THOMAS RANDOLPH | DRAWN·BY.
HUBERT REEVES

THE STAIR HALL

TUCKAHOE, GOOCHLAND COUNTY, VIRGINIA

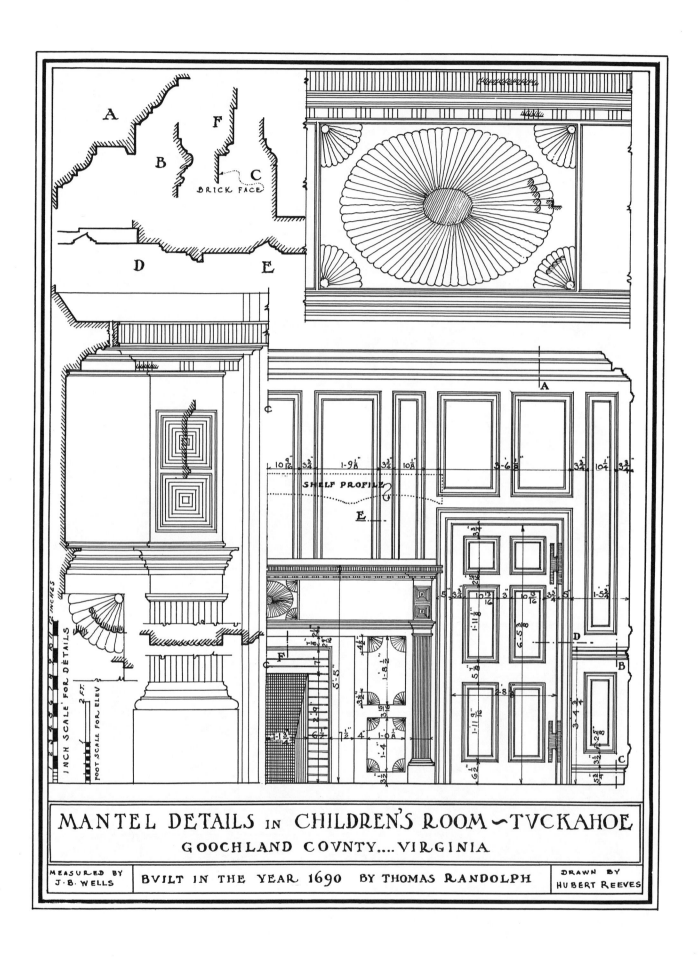

MANTEL DETAILS IN CHILDREN'S ROOM ~ TVCKAHOE

GOOCHLAND COVNTY.... VIRGINIA

MEASURED BY J·B·WELLS — BVILT IN THE YEAR 1690 BY THOMAS RANDOLPH — DRAWN BY HVBERT REEVES

DETAIL OF STAIR BRACKET

The woodwork in the stair hall in natural wood finish is almost unique
in this country, where paint was the rule in this period

TUCKAHOE, GOOCHLAND COUNTY, VIRGINIA

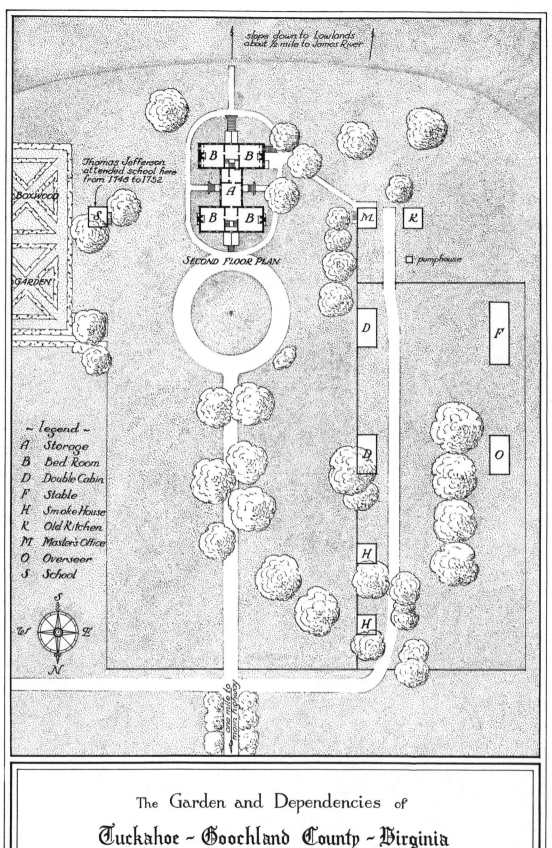

slope down to Lowlands
about ½ mile to James River

Thomas Jefferson
attended school here
from 1748 to 1752.

BOXWOOD

GARDEN

B B

A

B B

SECOND FLOOR PLAN

M R

□ pumphouse

D

F

D

O

H

H

~ Legend ~
A   Storage
B   Bed Room
D   Double Cabin
F   Stable
H   Smoke House
K   Old Kitchen
M   Master's Office
O   Overseer
S   School

one mile to main highway

The Garden and Dependencies of

Tuckahoe ~ Goochland County ~ Virginia

Built by   THOMAS RANDOLF   About 1690.

Graphic   25'   0'   25'   50'   75'   Scale.

76

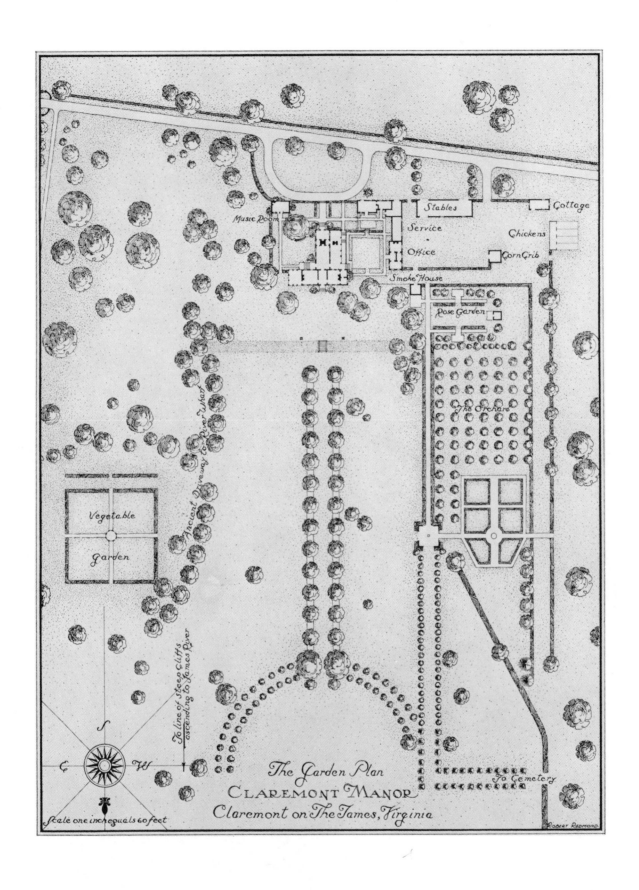

CLAREMONT MANOR, CLAREMONT–ON–THE–JAMES, VIRGINIA

THE FRONT DRIVEWAY AND ENTRANCE

CLAREMONT MANOR, CLAREMONT–ON–THE–JAMES, VIRGINIA

Now owned by General William H. Cocke

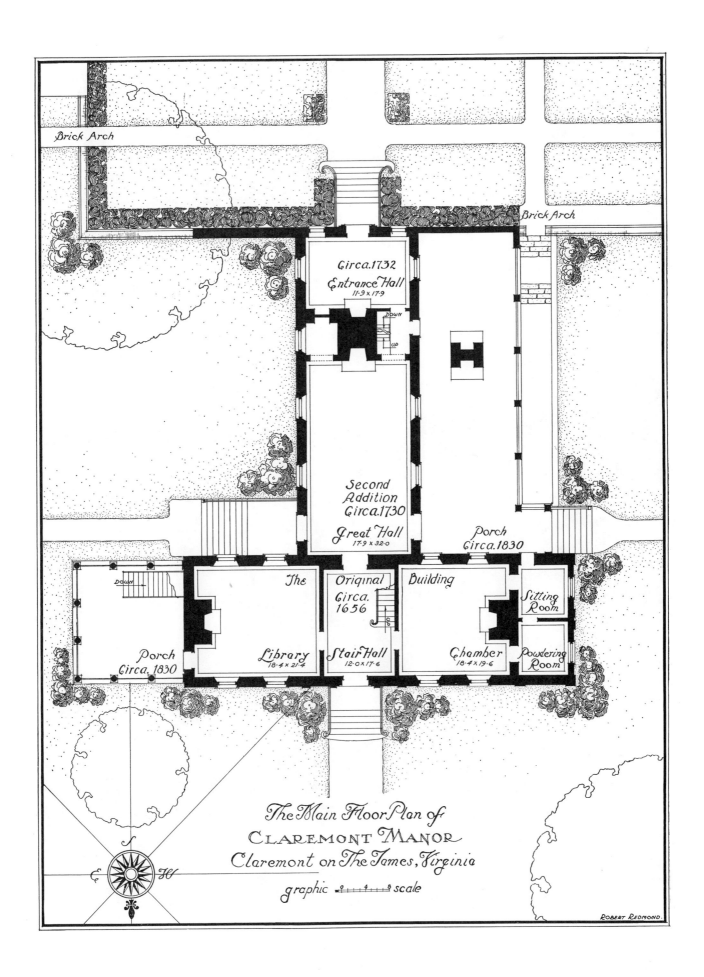

Brick Arch

Brick Arch

Circa. 1732
Entrance Hall
11-9 x 17-9

DOWN

UP

Second
Addition
Circa. 1730

Great Hall
17-9 x 32-0

Porch
Circa. 1830

DOWN

The

Original
Circa.
1656

Building

Sitting
Room

Porch
Circa. 1830

Library
18-4 x 21-4

Stair Hall
12-0 x 17-6

Chamber
18-4 x 19-6

Powdering
Room

The Main Floor Plan of
CLAREMONT MANOR
Claremont on The James, Virginia

graphic ⊢——⊢——⊢ scale

ROBERT REDMOND.

Photograph by Edward Pierrepont Beckwith

THE EAST COURTYARD

Half enclosed by the ancient quarters and offices and shaded by giant catalpa trees

CLAREMONT MANOR, CLAREMONT-ON-THE-JAMES, VIRGINIA

OLD SMOKE HOUSE AND SUNDIAL

CLAREMONT MANOR, CLAREMONT–ON–THE–JAMES, VIRGINIA

Restored 1928

Facade of CLAREM
facing The

MANOR Restored
mes River

actual scale ⅛" = 1'-0'
ROBERT REDMOND

83

Detail of the Entrance Doorway

CLAREMONT MANOR, CLAREMONT–ON–THE–JAMES, VIRGINIA

THE WESTERN OFFICE, ONE OF TWO WHICH FLANK THE FORECOURT

The connecting wall was rebuilt upon its original foundations in 1929

CLAREMONT MANOR, CLAREMONT–ON–THE–JAMES, VIRGINIA

Photograph by Edward Pierrepont Beckwith

The Great Hall

CLAREMONT MANOR, CLAREMONT–ON–THE–JAMES, VIRGINIA

Photographs by Edward Pierrepont Beckwith

THE STAIR HALL

THE LIBRARY

CLAREMONT MANOR, CLAREMONT–ON–THE–JAMES, VIRGINIA

Photograph by Edward Pierrepont Beckwith

The Garden Wing

CLAREMONT MANOR, CLAREMONT–ON–THE–JAMES, VIRGINIA

Photograph by H. Bagby

VIEW OF THE NORTHWEST FAÇADE FROM THE GARDEN

YORK HALL, YORKTOWN, VIRGINIA

North East Facade

York Hall - Yorktown - Virginia

Built by William Nelson in 1740

Restored by Capt. George P. Blow

Graphic Scale

Louis D. Carlo N.Y.

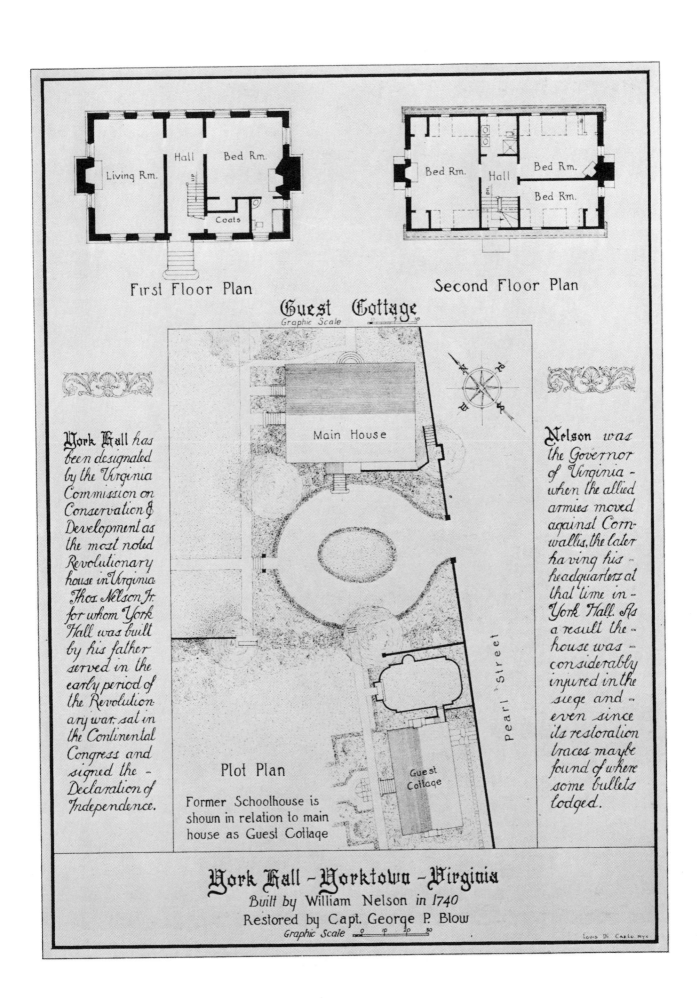

First Floor Plan

Living Rm.

Hall

Bed Rm.

Coats

Second Floor Plan

Bed Rm.

Hall

Bed Rm.

Bed Rm.

Guest Cottage
Graphic Scale

Main House

York Hall has been designated by the Virginia Commission on Conservation & Development as the most noted Revolutionary house in Virginia. Thos. Nelson Jr. for whom York Hall was built by his father served in the early period of the Revolutionary war, sat in the Continental Congress and signed the Declaration of Independence.

Nelson was the Governor of Virginia - when the allied armies moved against Cornwallis, the later having his headquarters at that time in York Hall. As a result the house was considerably injured in the siege and even since its restoration traces maybe found of where some bullets lodged.

Pearl Street

Plot Plan

Former Schoolhouse is shown in relation to main house as Guest Cottage

Guest Cottage

York Hall - Yorktown - Virginia
Built by William Nelson in 1740
Restored by Capt. George P. Blow
Graphic Scale

Louis Di Carlo Nyc

VIEW FROM THE FORECOURT

YORK HALL, YORKTOWN, VIRGINIA

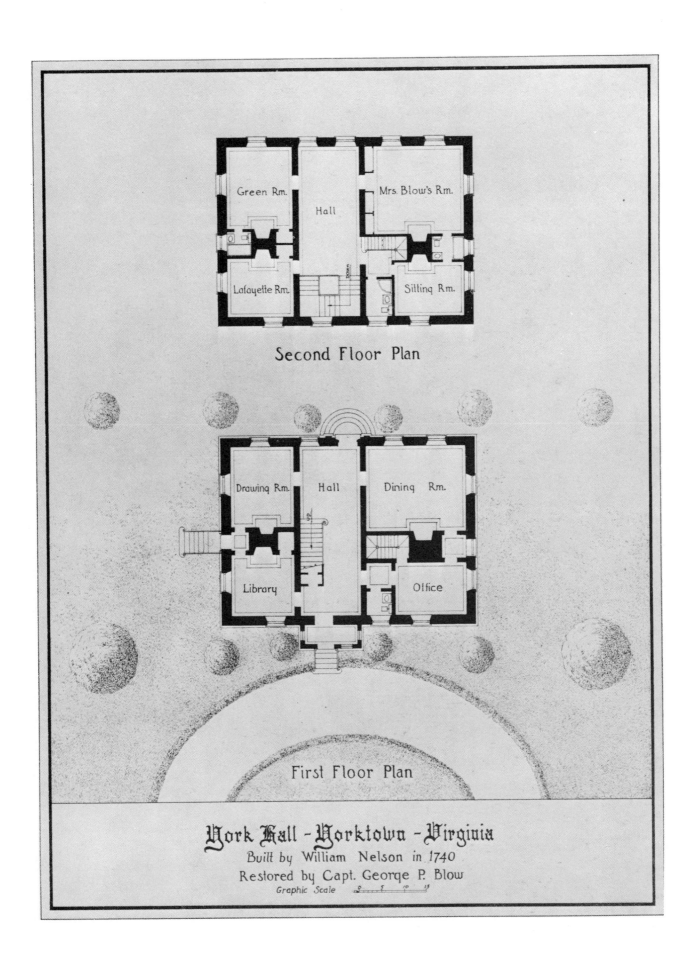

Second Floor Plan

First Floor Plan

York Hall - Yorktown - Virginia

Built by William Nelson in 1740

Restored by Capt. George P. Blow

Graphic Scale

Photograph by H. Bagby

VIEW FROM THE ROAD

YORK HALL, YORKTOWN, VIRGINIA

Photograph by H. Bagby

THE GUEST COTTAGE

Photograph by Robert W. Tebbs

VIEW FROM THE NORTHEAST

YORK HALL, YORKTOWN, VIRGINIA

95

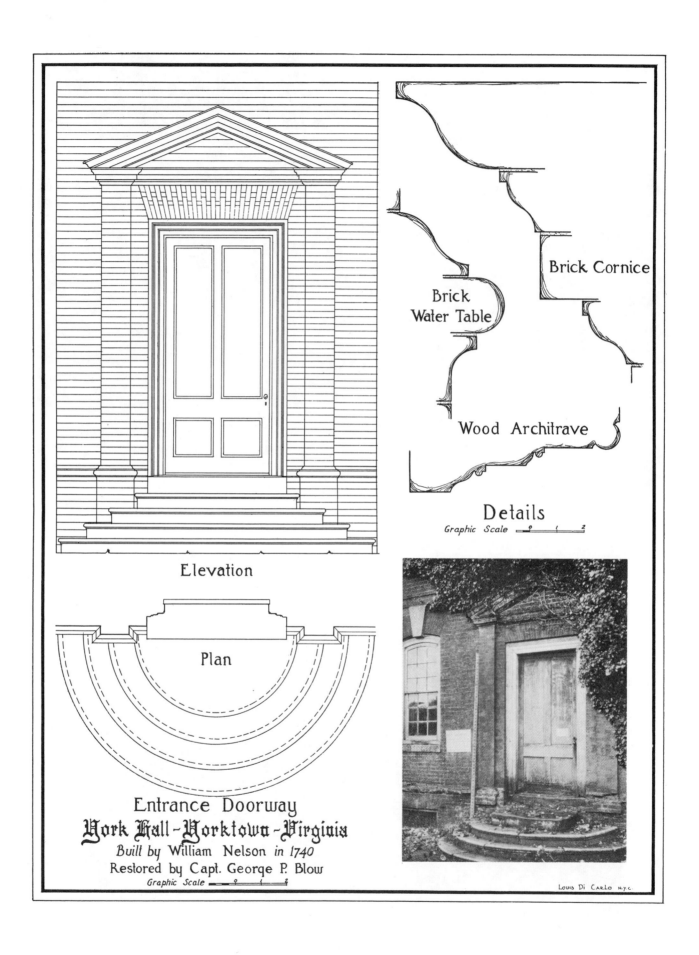

Elevation

Plan

Brick Cornice

Brick
Water Table

Wood Architrave

Details

Graphic Scale

Entrance Doorway
York Hall - Yorktown - Virginia
Built by William Nelson in 1740
Restored by Capt. George P. Blow
Graphic Scale

Louis Di Carlo N.Y.C.

A Portion of the Original Stair Rail Found in the Attic

Photographs by Robert W. Tebbs

Original Woodwork in the Dining Room

YORK HALL, YORKTOWN, VIRGINIA

The Dining Room

A Bedroom

YORK HALL, YORKTOWN, VIRGINIA

Photograph by Robert W. Tebbs

THE SOUTH FAÇADE

CARTER'S GROVE, WILLIAMSBURG, VIRGINIA

The River Side Entrance

CARTER'S GROVE, WILLIAMSBURG, VIRGINIA

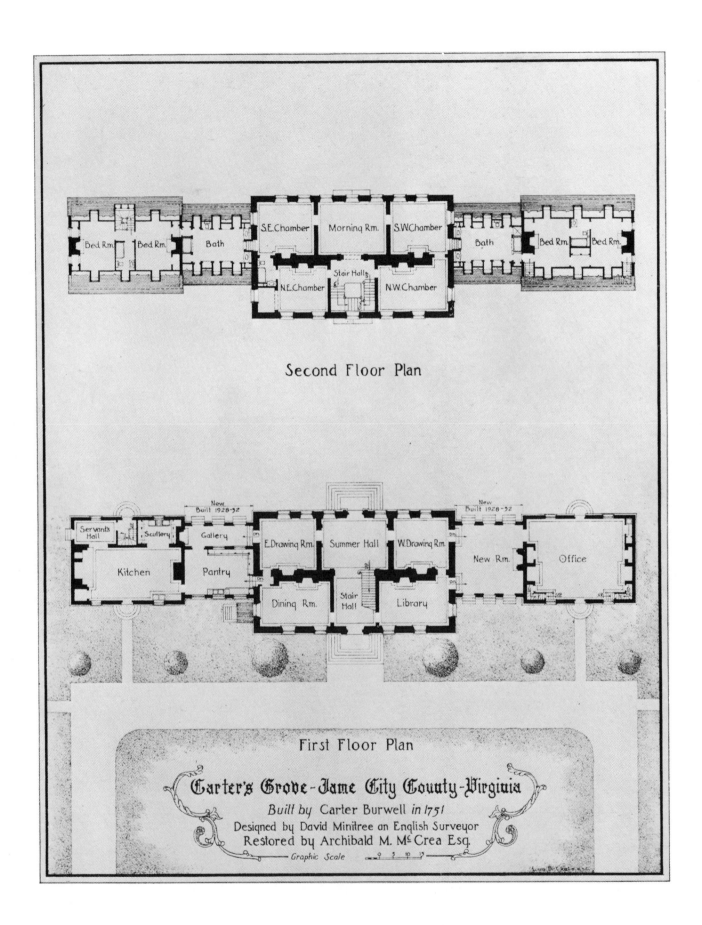

Second Floor Plan

First Floor Plan

Carter's Grove-Jame City County-Virginia

Built by Carter Burwell in 1751
Designed by David Minitree an English Surveyor
Restored by Archibald M. Mc Crea Esq.

Graphic Scale

South o
𝕮arter's 𝕲rove-J
Built by Ca
Designed by David
Restored by A
——— Graphic Sc

Facade

y County-Virginia

vell *in 1751*

English Surveyor

. Mc Crea Esq.

G.A. Mang.

THE DINING ROOM

Photographs by Robert W. Tebbs

THE WEST DRAWING ROOM

CARTER'S GROVE, WILLIAMSBURG, VIRGINIA

THE ENTRANCE HALL

DETAIL OF THE MAIN STAIRCASE

CARTER'S GROVE, WILLIAMSBURG, VIRGINIA

Photograph by Robert W. Tebbs

THE EAST DRAWING ROOM

CARTER'S GROVE, WILLIAMSBURG, VIRGINIA

PLOT·PLAN
WILTON-VIRGINIA

SCALE

WILTON–ON–THE–JAMES, VIRGINIA

107

The Entrance Facade
of WILTON on The James River Virginia
Drawn to The Scale of 1 in.=8 ft.

E.F. O'DWYER

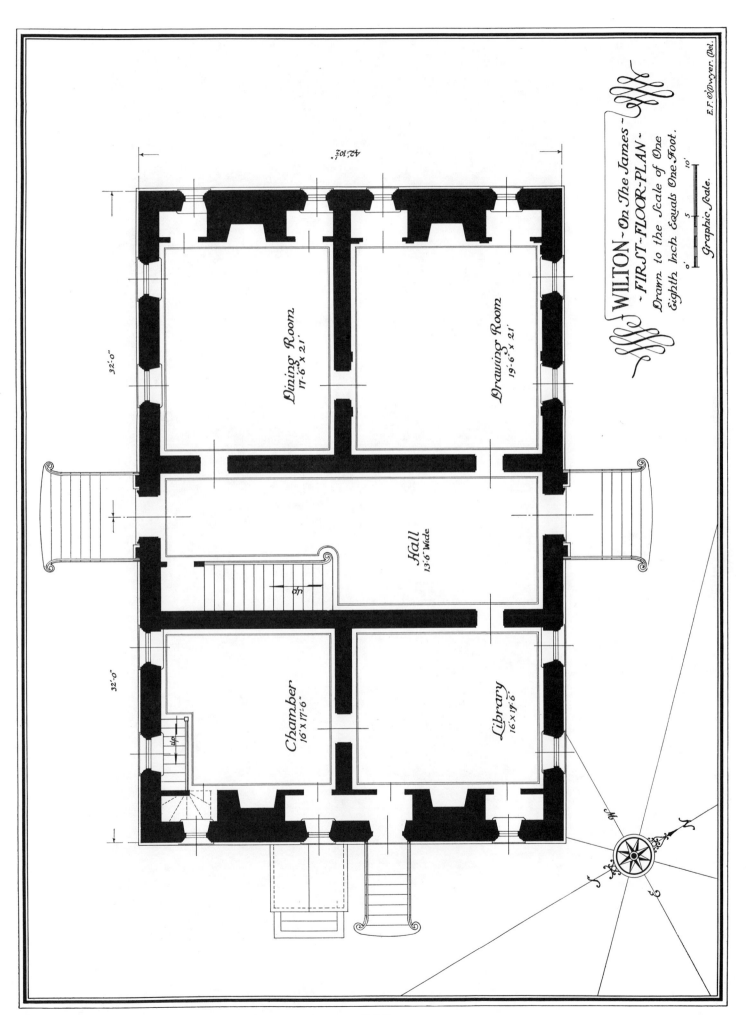

WILTON ~ On The James ~
~ FIRST ~ FLOOR ~ PLAN ~

*Drawn to the Scale of One
Eighth Inch Equals One Foot.*

E.F. O'Dwyer. Del.

Graphic Scale.

0'   5   10'

42'-10½"

Dining Room
17'-6" x 21'

Drawing Room
19'-6" x 21'

32'-0"

Hall
13'-6" Wide

Chamber
16' x 17'-6"

Library
16' x 19'-6"

32'-0"

VIEW FROM THE NORTHWEST

WILTON-ON-THE-JAMES, VIRGINIA

VIEW FROM THE SOUTH

WILTON-ON-THE-JAMES, VIRGINIA

DETAIL OF THE WEST DOOR

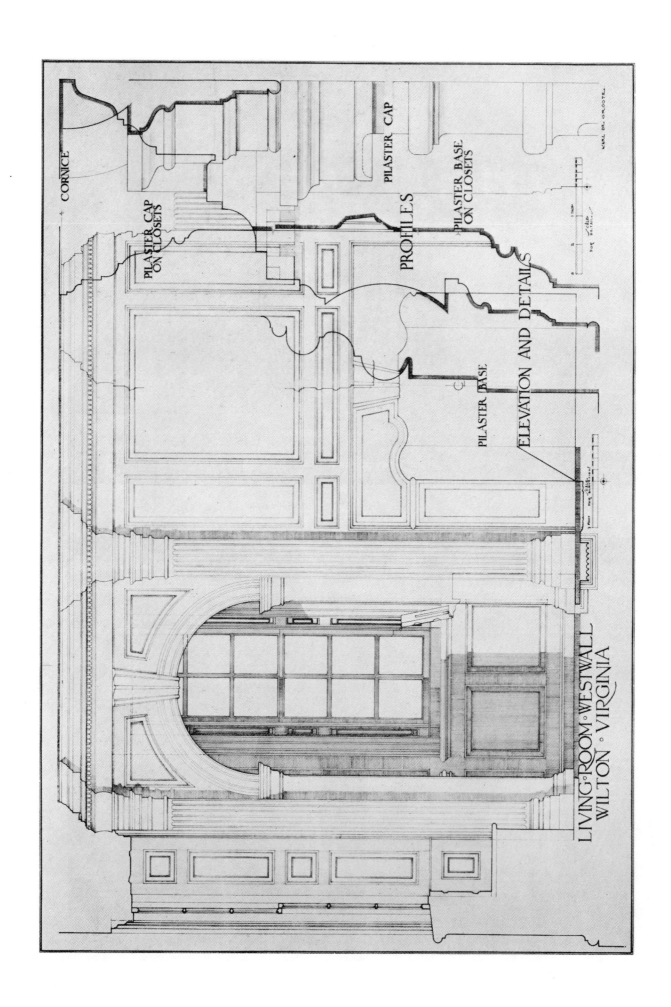

CORNICE

PILASTER CAP ON CLOSETS

PILASTER CAP

PILASTER BASE ON CLOSETS

PROFILES

PILASTER BASE ON CLOSETS

PILASTER BASE

ELEVATION AND DETAILS

KARL DE. GROOTE.

LIVING·ROOM·WEST·WALL
WILTON · VIRGINIA

The Fireplace in the East Room

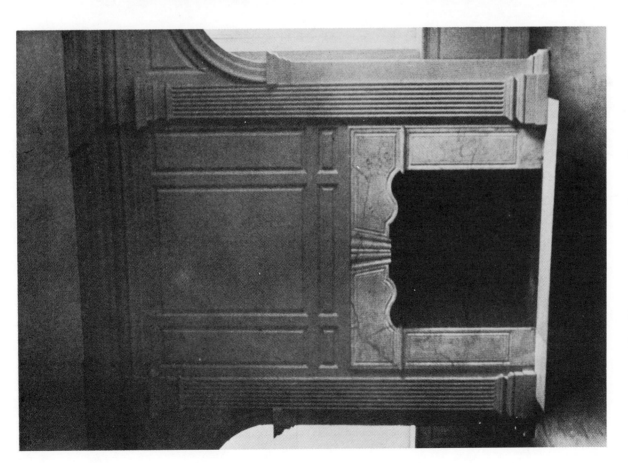

The Fireplace in the Living Room

WILTON–ON–THE–JAMES, VIRGINIA

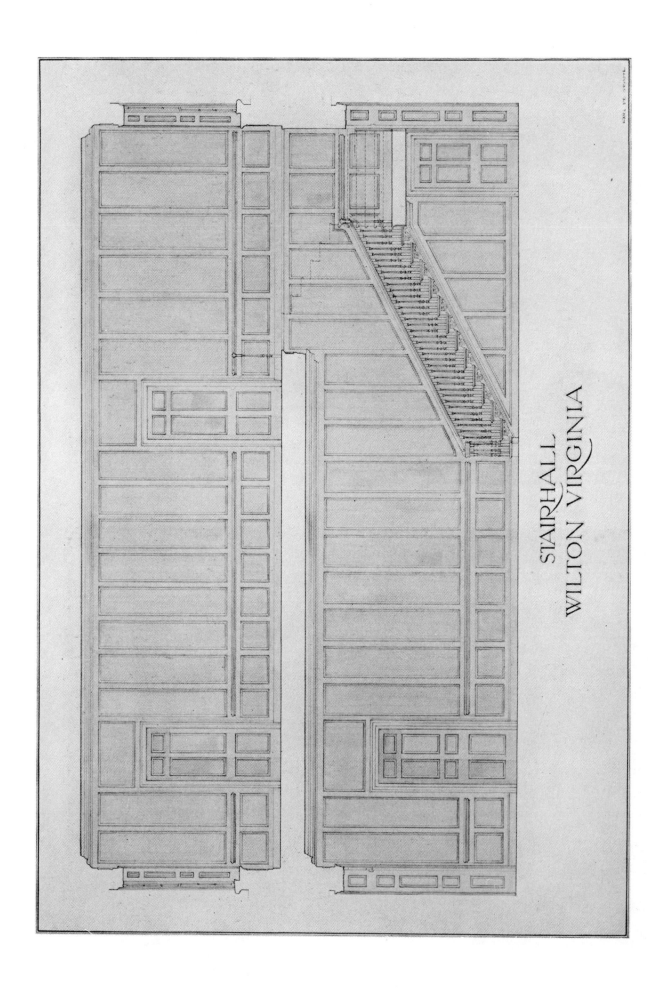

STAIRHALL
WILTON VIRGINIA

DETAIL OF THE MAIN STAIRCASE

WILTON-ON-THE-JAMES, VIRGINIA

THE MAIN STAIRCASE

THE DINING
ROOM OF
WILTON

Below, this
inscription
was found on
the back of a
cornice during
the recent
restoration:

"*Samson
Darril put up
this cornish in
the year of our
Lord 1753.*"

Photograph by James Ross Gillie

Second-Story Central Window of Main Façade

THE BRICE HOUSE, ANNAPOLIS, MARYLAND

The MAIN FACADE of

The Price House ~ Annapolis ~ Maryland

(as restored.)

Built in 1740

Scale of Feet

0   10   20   30   40

Hugh A. Simpson Del.

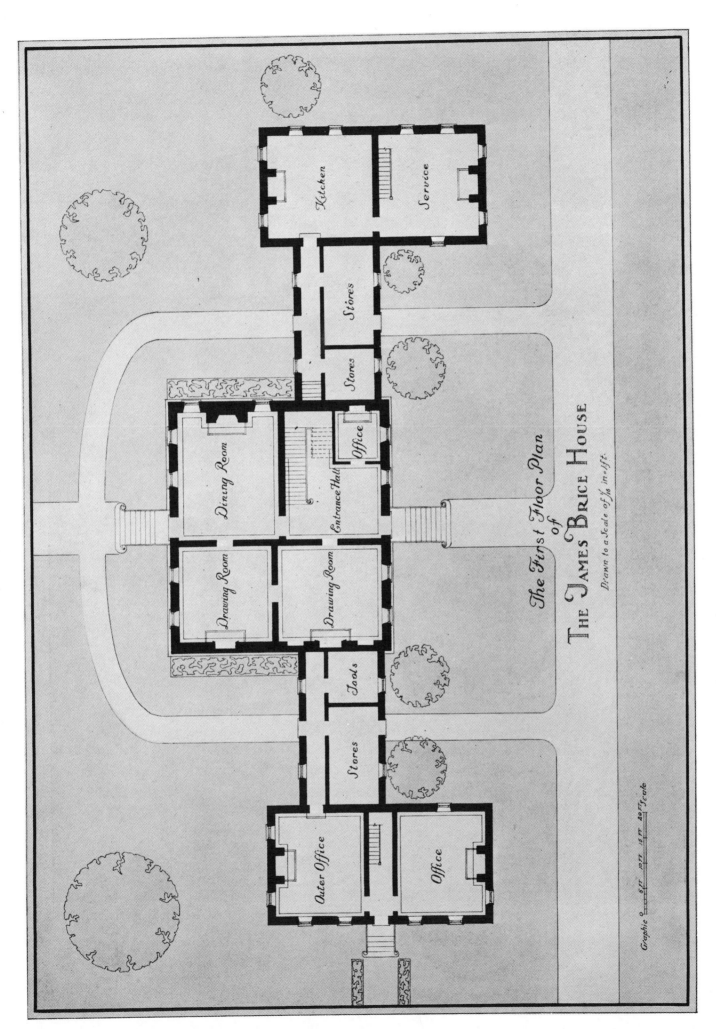

Kitchen

Service

Stores

Stores

Dining Room

Entrance Hall

Office

Drawing Room

Drawing Room

Tools

Stores

Outer Office

Office

The First Floor Plan
of
THE JAMES BRICE HOUSE

Drawn to a Scale of ⅟₁₆ in = 1 ft.

Graphic Scale

Courtesy of the Monograph Series. Photograph by Kenneth Clark

THE BRICE HOUSE, ANNAPOLIS, MARYLAND

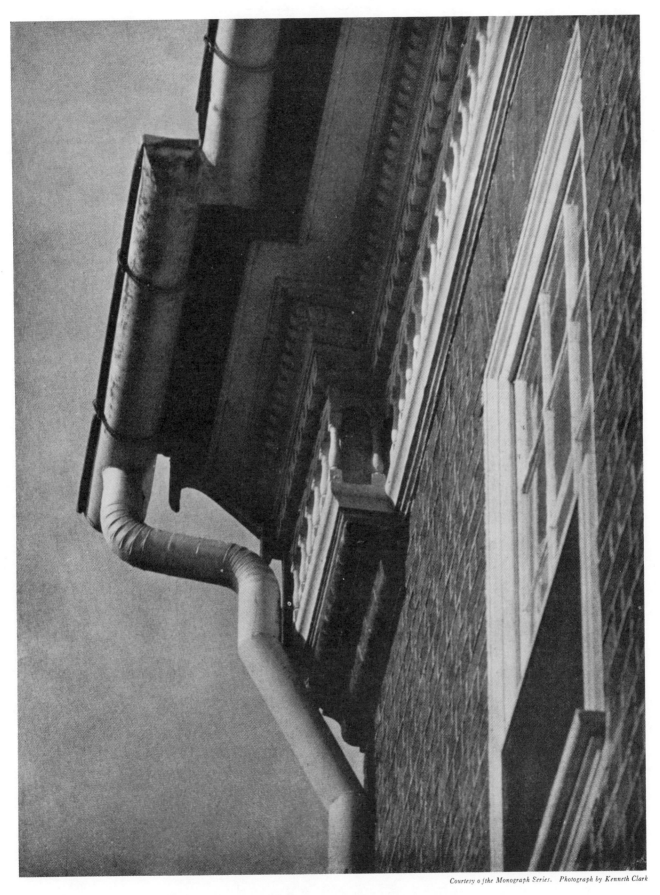

DETAIL OF THE CORNICE

THE BRICE HOUSE, ANNAPOLIS, MARYLAND

Mantle Side of Dining Room

THE JAMES BRICE HOUSE

Annapolis, Maryland.
½ inch = 1 foot

Scale

L. P. Rixford del.

Details of Mantel

THE BRICE HOUSE, ANNAPOLIS, MARYLAND

Courtesy of the Monograph Series.   Photograph by Kenneth Clark

INTERIOR CORNICE DETAIL

THE BRICE HOUSE, ANNAPOLIS, MARYLAND

Courtesy of the Monograph Series.   Photograph by Kenneth Clark

A STAIRCASE DETAIL

THE BRICE HOUSE, ANNAPOLIS, MARYLAND

Mantle End of Parlour

THE JAMES BRICE HOUSE

Annapolis, Maryland.

½ inch = 1 foot

Scale

L. L. Rixford del.

THE DINING ROOM

THE BRICE HOUSE, ANNAPOLIS, MARYLAND

AN INTERIOR CORNICE DETAIL

THE BRICE HOUSE, ANNAPOLIS, MARYLAND

Photograph by Robert W. Tebbs

The North Portico

TULIP HILL, ANNE ARUNDEL COUNTY, MARYLAND

For the exterior Walls English
Facing Brick was probably
imported, laid Flemish Bond
in the Main House, American
Bond in the later built Wings.

The North or

Tulip Hill ~ Anne A

Graphic 5

...ance Facade.

...el County ~ Maryland.

...° ___15___ ...h Scale.

The Roofs on the connecting Wings shown here at original Height have recently been raised, and the Wood Shingles on all the Roofs replaced with Slate.

Louis Koefoed. Del.

The Entrance Façade from the North

TULIP HILL, ANNE ARUNDEL COUNTY, MARYLAND

THE SOUTH FAÇADE

TULIP HILL, ANNE ARUNDEL COUNTY, MARYLAND

133

DETAIL OF THE EAST WING

DETAIL OF THE SOUTH ENTRANCE

TULIP HILL, ANNE ARUNDEL COUNTY, MARYLAND

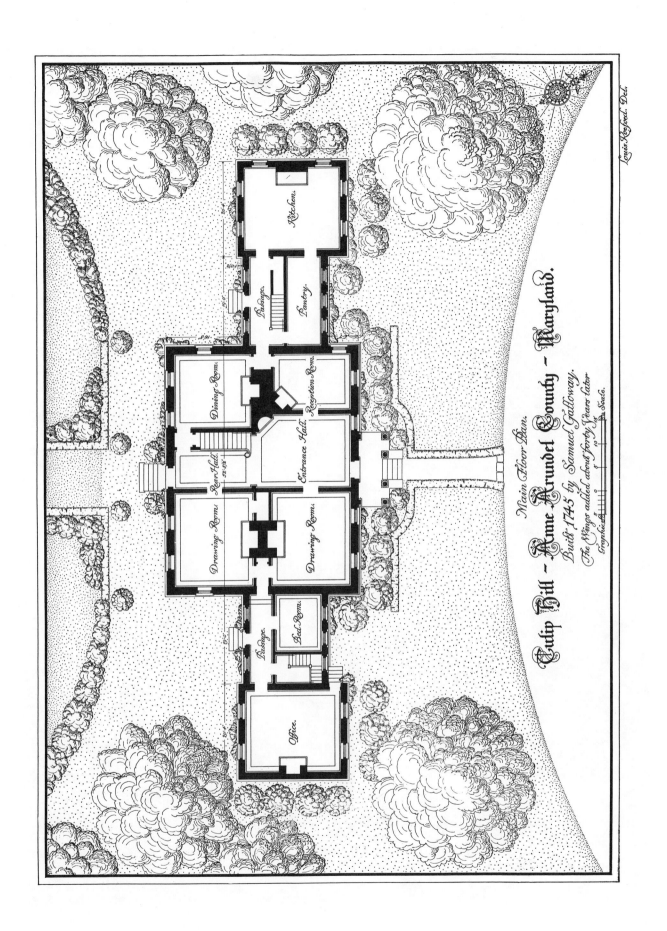

Main Floor Plan.

Tulip Hill ~ Anne Arundel County ~ Maryland.

Built 1745 by Samuel Galloway.

The Wings added about Forty Years later.

Graphic Scale.

Louis Reyfoed. Del.

Photograph by Robert W. Tebbs

The Corner Cupboard and Staircase in the Entrance Hall
TULIP HILL, ANNE ARUNDEL COUNTY, MARYLAND

Plan

Scale

Archivolt

Impost

Scale of Details
Inches

*Octagon House
The Entrance*

Scale of Elevation
Feet & Inches

OCTAGON HOUSE, WASHINGTON, D. C.

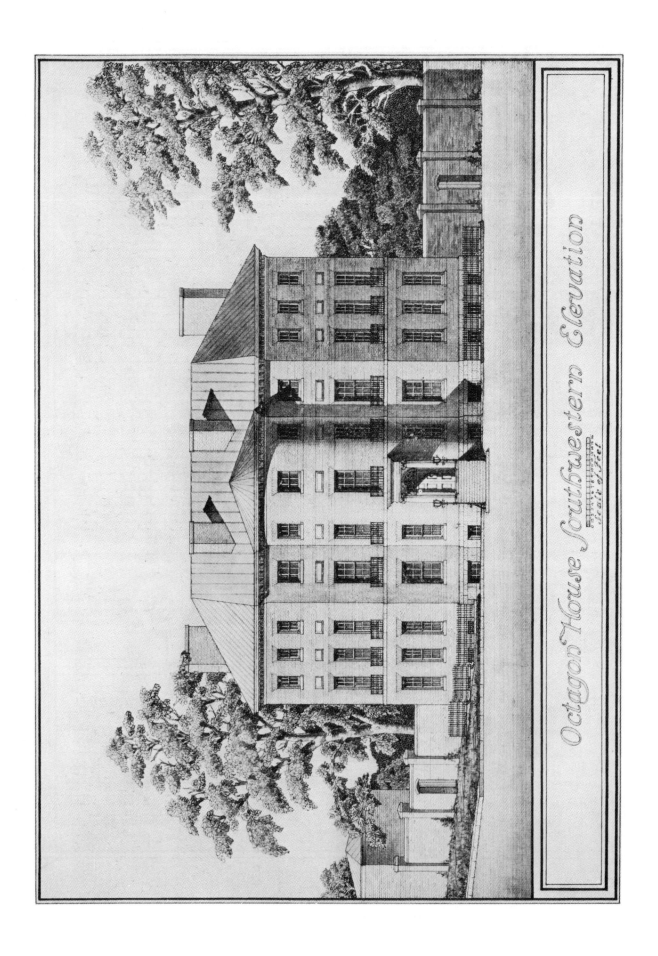

Octagon House Southwestern Elevation

Scale of Feet

VIEW FROM THE SOUTHWEST

OCTAGON HOUSE, WASHINGTON, D. C.

Designed by William Thornton, and built 1798–1800

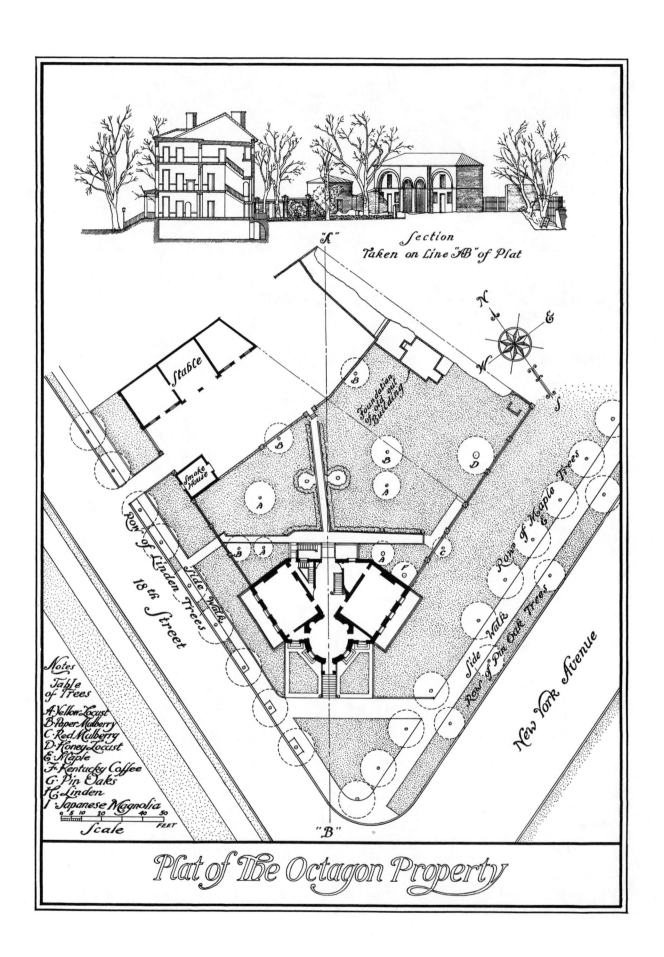

Section
Taken on Line "AB" of Plat

"A"

N
E
W
S

Stable

Foundation of old out Building

Smoke House

"B"

Row of Maple Trees

Side Walk

Row of Pin Oak Trees

New York Avenue

Row of Linden Trees

Side Walk

18th Street

Notes
Table
of Trees

A. Yellow Locust
B. Paper Mulberry
C. Red Mulberry
D. Honey Locust
E. Maple
F. Kentucky Coffee
G. Pin Oaks
H. Linden
I. Japanese Magnolia

0 5 10 20   40 50
FEET
Scale

Plat of The Octagon Property

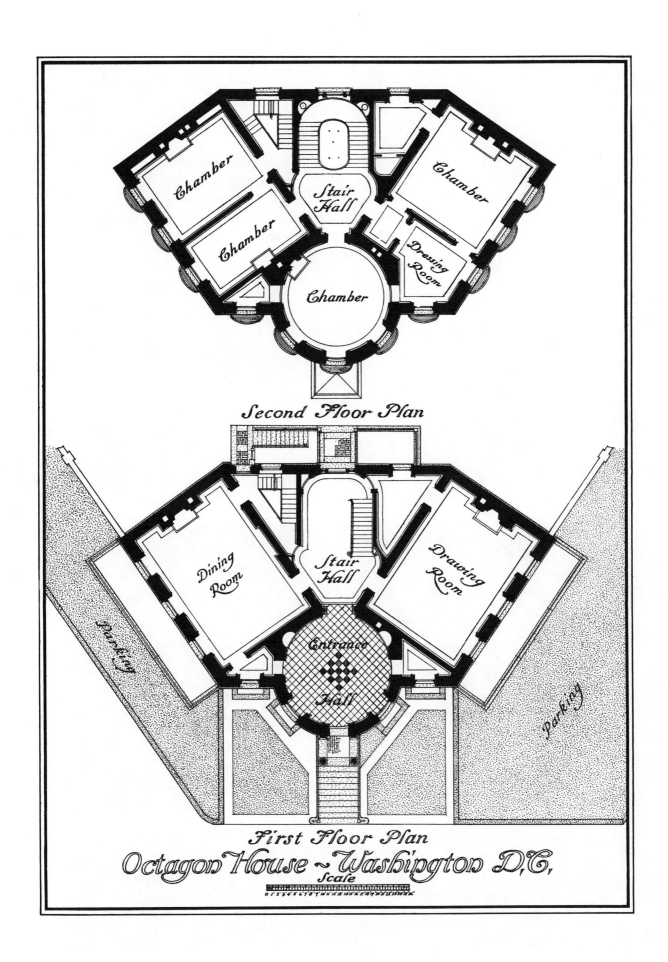

Second Floor Plan

First Floor Plan
Octagon House ~ Washington D.C.
Scale

DETAIL OF FIREPLACE

DETAIL OF FIREPLACE

OCTAGON HOUSE, WASHINGTON, D. C.

Detail of a Column Capital in the Entrance Hall

The Entrance Hall

OCTAGON HOUSE, WASHINGTON, D. C.

Scale
of Elevation
0" 3" 6" 9" 12"
Inches

Octagon House
Dining Room Mantel

Scale
of Details
0" 1" 2" 3"
Inches

East or Street Facade

Read House - New Castle - Delaware

The railing of the steps is a conjectural restoration

Graphic Scale

THE READ HOUSE, NEW CASTLE, DELAWARE

145

Courtesy of the Monograph Series. Photographs by Kenneth Clark

The Palladian Window in the East Façade

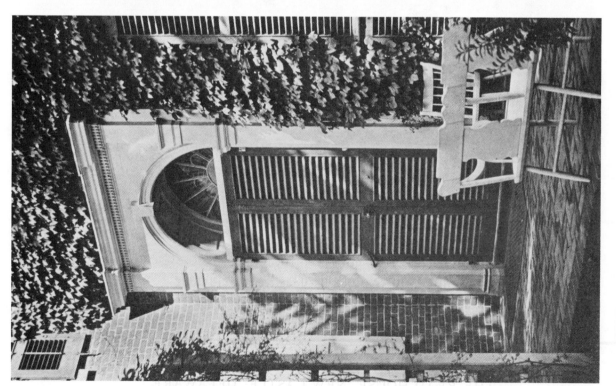

Side Entrance Doorway

THE READ HOUSE, NEW CASTLE, DELAWARE

146

Photograph by Courtland D. V. Hubbard

VIEW FROM THE EAST

THE READ HOUSE, NEW CASTLE, DELAWARE

147

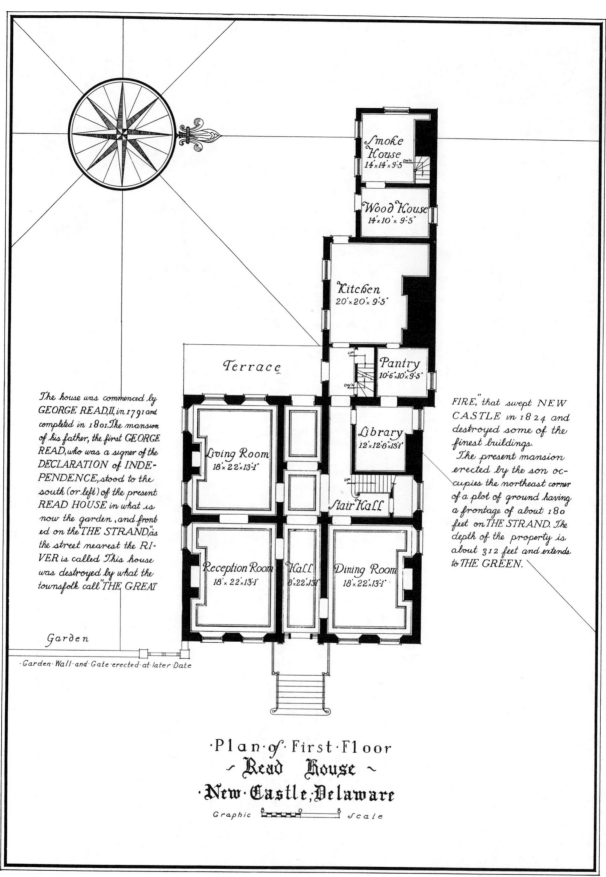

The house was commenced by GEORGE READ, II, in 1791 and completed in 1801. The mansion of his father, the first GEORGE READ, who was a signer of the DECLARATION of INDE-PENDENCE, stood to the south (or left) of the present READ HOUSE in what is now the garden, and front-ed on the "THE STRAND," as the street nearest the RI-VER is called. This house was destroyed by what the townsfolk call "THE GREAT

FIRE," that swept NEW CASTLE in 1824 and destroyed some of the finest buildings.

The present mansion erected by the son oc-cupies the northeast corner of a plot of ground having a frontage of about 180 feet on THE STRAND. The depth of the property is about 312 feet and extends to THE GREEN.

Smoke House
14'×14'×9'-5"

Wood House
14'×10'×9'-5"

Kitchen
20'×20'×9'-5"

Pantry
10'6"×10'×9'-5"

Library
12'×12'-6"×13'-1"

Living Room
18'×22'×13'-1"

Stair Hall

Terrace

Reception Room
18'×22'×13'-1"

Hall
8'×22'×13'-1"

Dining Room
18'×22'×13'-1"

Garden

·Garden·Wall·and·Gate·erected·at·later·Date

·Plan·of·First·Floor
~ Read House ~
·New·Castle, Delaware

Graphic   Scale

Philip Sanfilippo Del.

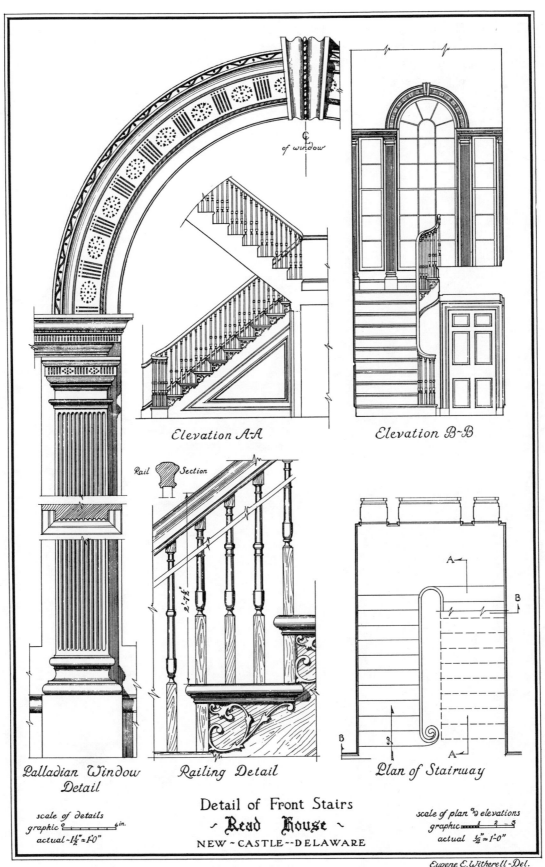

Elevation A-A

Elevation B-B

Rail Section

2'-7½"

Palladian Window
Detail

Railing Detail

Plan of Stairway

Detail of Front Stairs
~ Read House ~
NEW ~ CASTLE ~ DELAWARE

scale of details
graphic
actual ~ 1½" = 1'-0"

scale of plan ~ elevations
graphic
actual ~ ¼" = 1'-0"

Eugene E. Witherell - Del.

Courtesy of the Monograph Series.   Photograph by Kenneth Clark

AN ARCHWAY DETAIL

THE READ HOUSE, NEW CASTLE, DELAWARE

A MANTEL DETAIL

THE READ HOUSE, NEW CASTLE, DELAWARE

Courtesy of the Monograph Series. Photographs by Kenneth Clark

A STAIRCASE DETAIL

THE READ HOUSE, NEW CASTLE, DELAWARE

DETAIL OF A DOOR IN THE FIRST-STORY HALL

Photograph by Frances Benjamin Johnston

Detail of the West Porch

SWANWICK MANOR, FARNHURST, DELAWARE

The West Elevation
Swanwick Manor
A Regency House

Landers Lane, Farnhurst, Delaware

graphic scale   ⅛″=1′0″ actual scale

The East Elevation
Swantwick Manor
A Regency House

Landers Lane. Farnhurst Delaware

graphic scale   ⅛"=1'0" actual scale

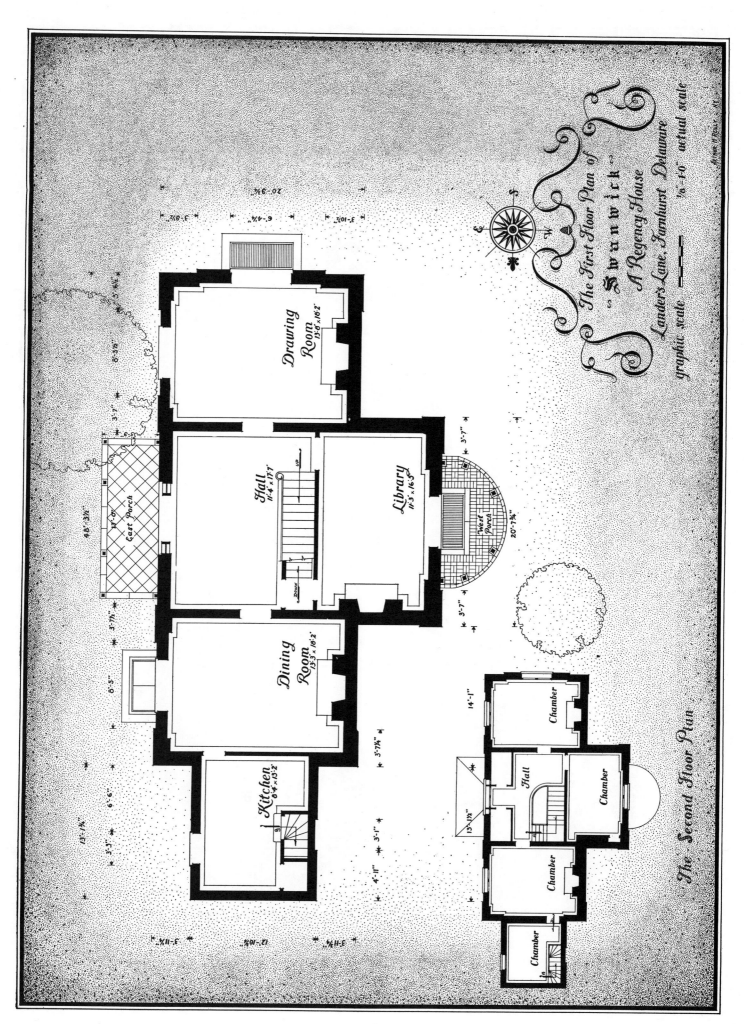

The First Floor Plan of
"Swanwick"
A Regency House
Lander's Lane, Farnhurst, Delaware
graphic scale — ⅛" = 1'-0" actual scale

Drawing Room
13'-6" x 16'-2"

Hall
11'-4" x 17'-1"

UP

Library
11'-3" x 16'-5"

West Porch

East Porch

Dining Room
13'-3" x 16'-2"

Kitchen
10'-4" x 13'-2"

Chamber

Hall

Chamber

Chamber

Chamber

Chamber

The Second Floor Plan

Photograph by Frances Benjamin Johnston

VIEW FROM THE WEST

SWANWICK MANOR, FARNHURST, DELAWARE

Photograph by Frances Benjamin Johnston

The East Façade

SWANWICK MANOR, FARNHURST, DELAWARE

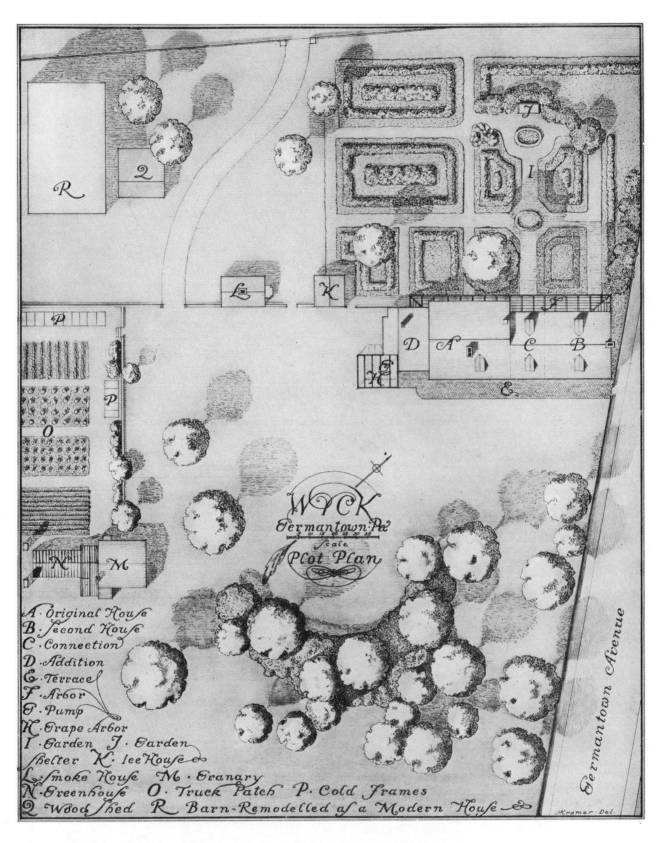

A · Original House
B · Second House
C · Connection
D · Addition
E · Terrace
F · Arbor
G · Pump
H · Grape Arbor
I · Garden J · Garden
Shelter K · Ice House
L · Smoke House M · Granary
N · Greenhouse O · Truck Patch P · Cold Frames
Q · Wood Shed R · Barn—Remodelled as a Modern House

WYCK
Germantown Pa
Scale
Plot Plan

Germantown Avenue

WYCK, GERMANTOWN, PENNSYLVANIA

Photographs by Phil B. Wallace

DETAIL OF THE DOOR ON THE TERRACE

VIEW ALONG THE TERRACE ON THE NORTHWEST SIDE

WYCK, GERMANTOWN, PENNSYLVANIA

The Northwest Façade

WYCK, GERMANTOWN, PENNSYLVANIA

W
Germa
First portion at W
Alterations made by

Penn.

erected about 1690.

m Strickland in 1824.

H Kramer Del.

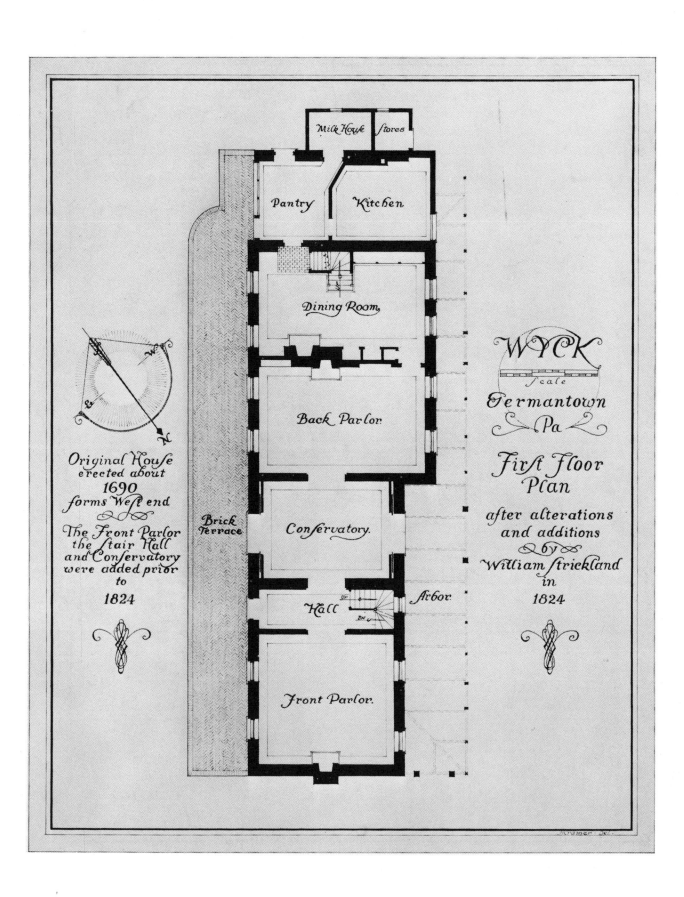

Milk House   stores

Pantry   Kitchen

Dining Room,

Back Parlor

Brick Terrace

Conservatory.

Original House
erected about
1690
forms West end

The Front Parlor
the Stair Hall
and Conservatory
were added prior
to
1824

Hall   Arbor

Front Parlor.

WYCK
scale
Germantown
Pa

First Floor
Plan

after alterations
and additions
by
William Strickland
in
1824

THE GENERAL LEAVENWORTH MANSION, SYRACUSE, NEW YORK

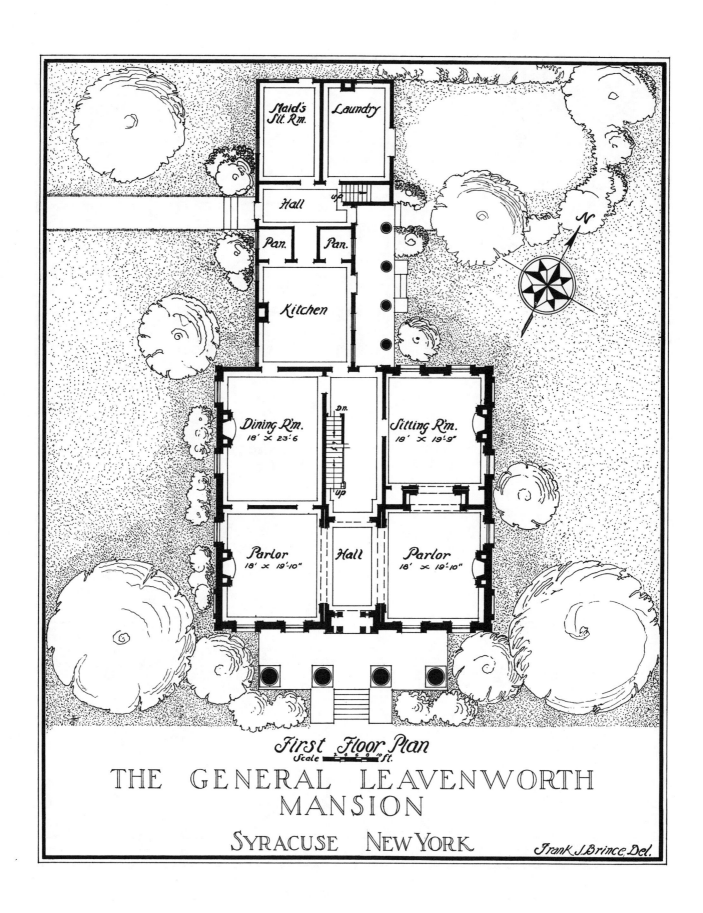

Maid's Sit. Rm.

Laundry

Hall

up

Pan.

Pan.

Kitchen

N

Dining R'm.
18' × 23'6

Dn.

up

Sitting R'm.
18' × 19'9"

Parlor
18' × 19'-10"

Hall

Parlor
18' × 19'-10"

First Floor Plan
Scale

THE GENERAL LEAVENWORTH
MANSION

SYRACUSE   NEW YORK

Frank J. Brince Del.

THE SOUTH FRONT

THE GENERAL LEAVENWORTH MANSION, SYRACUSE, NEW YORK

VIEW FROM THE SOUTHWEST

THE GENERAL LEAVENWORTH MANSION, SYRACUSE, NEW YORK

Section B

Section A

Section C

Grille in Main Cornice

Scale [_____] Inches

Front Window

Main Entrance

Section

Exterior Details

GENERAL LEAVENWORTH MANSION

SYRACVSE NEW YORK

Scale of Details [_____] Feet

Inches Scale of Sections

MORRIS JACKSON · DEL·

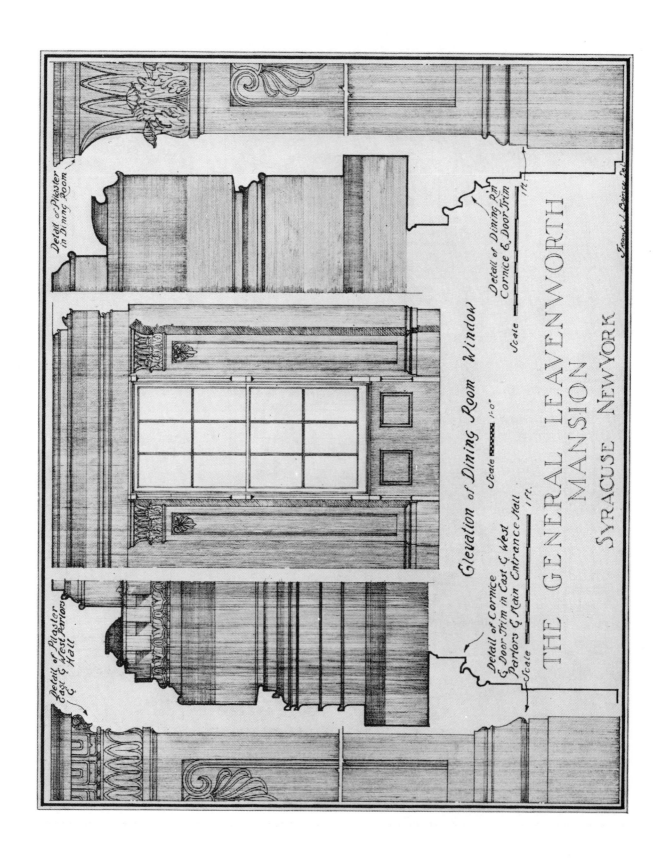

Detail of Plaster in Dining Room

Detail of Dining Rm Cornice & Door Trim

Scale

Elevation of Dining Room Window

Scale

Detail of Plaster East & West Parlors & Hall

Detail of Cornice & Door Trim in East & West Parlors & Main Entrance Hall

Scale

Frank J. Prince Del.

THE GENERAL LEAVENWORTH MANSION

Syracuse New York

DETAIL OF THE GARDEN FRONT

CLERMONT, LIVINGSTON MANOR, TIVOLI–ON–THE–HUDSON, NEW YORK

Clermont Livingston Manor

Built in 1730 by Robert Livingston, son of the first Lord of the Manor
Burned by British 1777 – Rebuilt 1718

As the House Appeared in 1870

CLERMONT, LIVINGSTON MANOR, TIVOLI–ON–THE–HUDSON, NEW YORK

Photograph by Courtland V. D. Hubbard

CLERMONT, LIVINGSTON MANOR, TIVOLI–ON–THE–HUDSON, NEW YORK

First Floor Plan

CLERMONT LIVINGSTON MANOR

Tivoli on the Hudson, New York.
Rebuilt Circa – 1778
Architect Unknown

Scale in feet
0   5   10   15   20

G. L. GERMAIN Jr. Del.

Photograph by Courtland V. D. Hubbard

THE ENTRANCE PORCH

CLERMONT, LIVINGSTON MANOR, TIVOLI-ON-THE-HUDSON, NEW YORK

South Elevation

North Elevation

graphic scale
0'   5'   10'   15'   20'

Marshall House
Rodman's Neck   New York.
The house originally styled "Hawkswood"
was erected about 1820
for L.R. Marshall Esq.

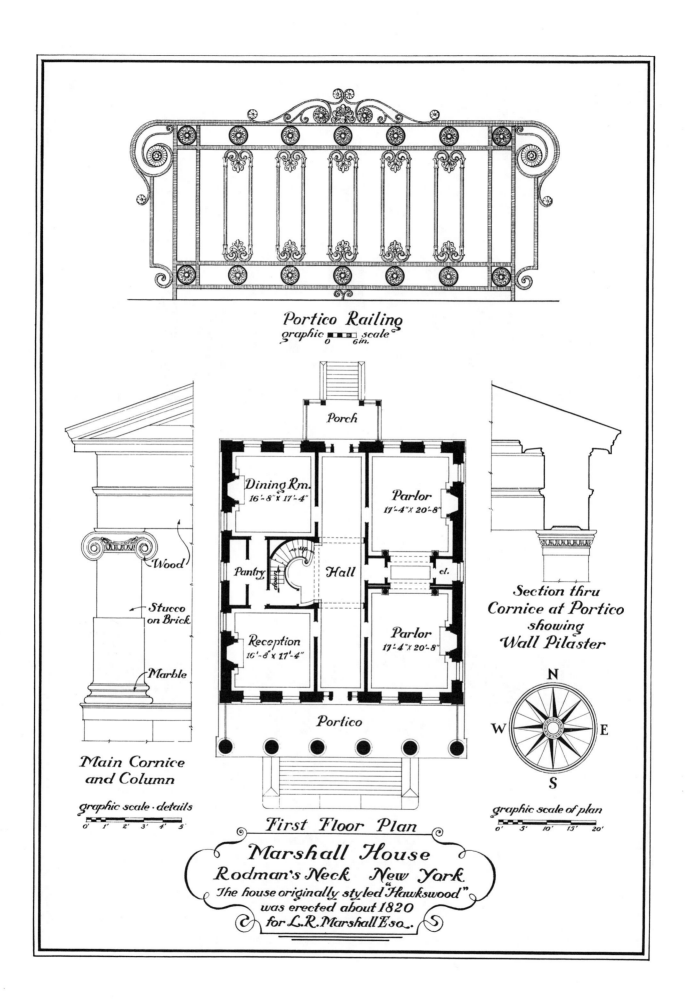

Portico Railing

graphic scale
0   6 in.

Porch

Dining Rm.
16'-8" x 17'-4"

Parlor
17'-4" x 20'-8"

Pantry

Hall

cl.

Reception
16'-8" x 17'-4"

Parlor
17'-4" x 20'-8"

Portico

Wood

Stucco
on Brick

Marble

Main Cornice
and Column

graphic scale · details
0' 1' 2' 3' 4' 5'

Section thru
Cornice at Portico
showing
Wall Pilaster

N

W   E

S

graphic scale of plan
0' 5' 10' 15' 20'

First Floor Plan

Marshall House
Rodman's Neck   New York.
The house originally styled "Hawkswood"
was erected about 1820
for L.R. Marshall Esq.

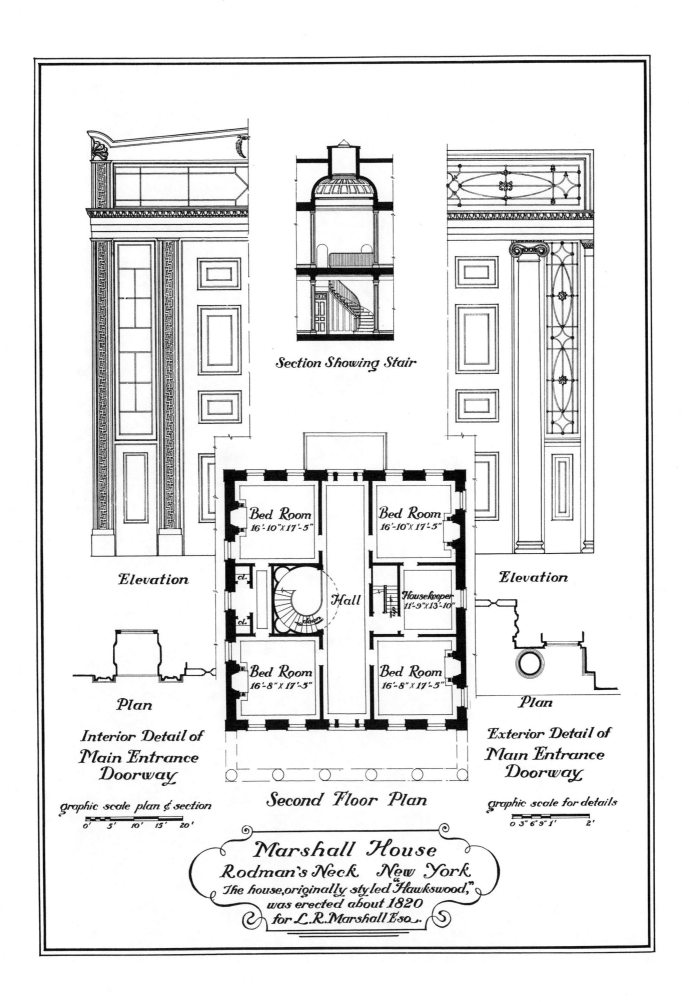

Elevation

Section Showing Stair

Elevation

Plan

Plan

Interior Detail of
Main Entrance
Doorway

Exterior Detail of
Main Entrance
Doorway

graphic scale plan & section

0'   5'   10'   15'   20'

Bed Room
16'-10"x 17'-5"

Bed Room
16'-10"x 17'-5"

cl.

Hall

Housekeeper
11'-9"x 13'-10"

cl.

Bed Room
16'-8"x 17'-5"

Bed Room
16'-8"x 17'-5"

Second Floor Plan

graphic scale for details

0 3" 6" 9" 1'   2'

Marshall House
Rodman's Neck   New York
The house, originally styled "Hawkswood,"
was erected about 1820
for L. R. Marshall Esq.

Courtesy of the New York City Department of Parks

THE SOUTH FAÇADE

MARSHALL HOUSE, RODMAN'S NECK, NEW YORK

Photographs courtesy of the New York City Department of Parks

Doorway in the First-floor Hall

The Main Staircase, First Floor

MARSHALL HOUSE, RODMAN'S NECK, NEW YORK

DETAIL OF THE VERANDA RAILING

DETAIL OF THE VERANDA CAPITALS

MARSHALL HOUSE, RODMAN'S NECK, NEW YORK

VIEW FROM THE SOUTH

THE NATHAN ROBERTS HOUSE, CANASTOTA, NEW YORK

SOVTH FACADE
of
THE NATHAN ROBERTS HOVSE
Genesee Tvrnpike - Canastota
New York

Scale

feet

Detail of Exterior
Cornice and Capital

A

B

Section   Interior   Exterior
Elevation

Scale ⊢⊢⊢⊢⊢ 0   1   2   3   4   5 feet

MAIN ENTRANCE
DETAILS
of
THE
NATHAN ROBERTS
HOVSE
Genesee Tvrnpike - Canastota
New York

Scale for Details
⊢⊢⊢⊢⊢ 0   1   2   3   4 Inches

Morris Jackson - Del -

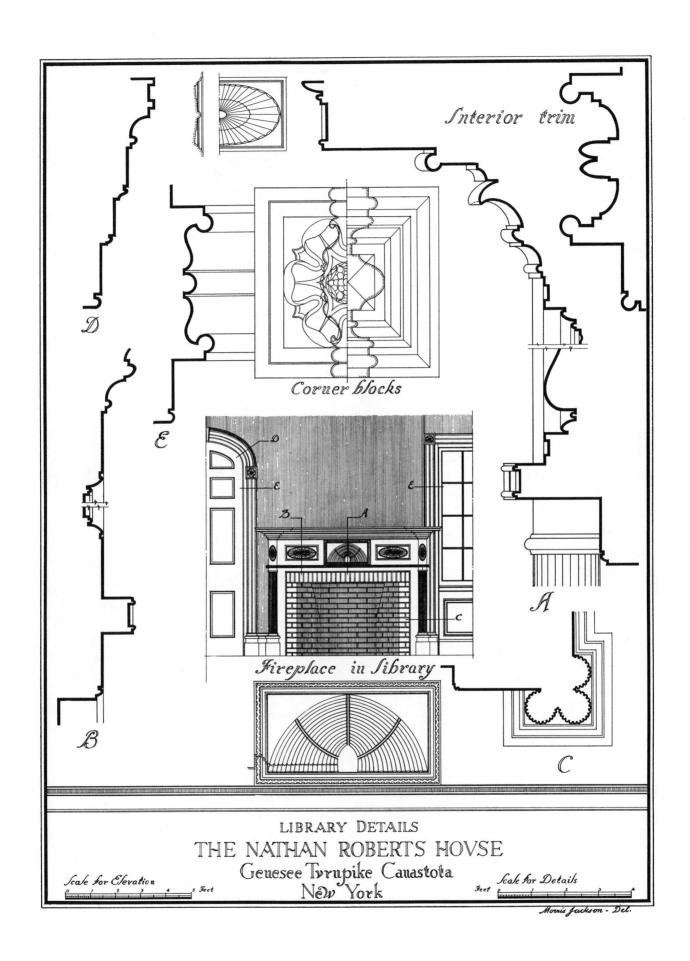

Interior trim

Corner blocks

Fireplace in Library

LIBRARY DETAILS
THE NATHAN ROBERTS HOVSE
Genesee Tvrupike Canastota
New York

Scale for Elevation

Scale for Details

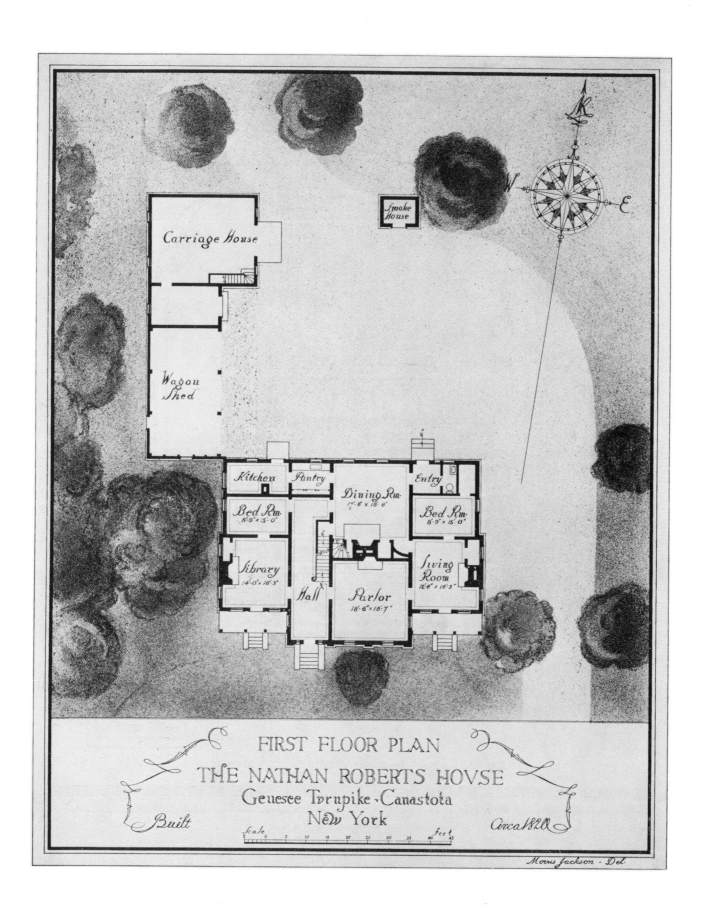

FIRST FLOOR PLAN

THE NATHAN ROBERTS HOVSE

Genesee Tvrnpike • Canastota
New York

Built   Circa 1820

Carriage House

Wagon
Shed

Smoke
House

Kitchen   Pantry   Dining Rm·
17'-8" x 18'-6"   Entry

Bed Rm·
8'-9" x 15'-0"   Bed Rm·
8'-9" x 15'-0"

Library
14'-0" x 16'-3"   Living
Room
16'-6" x 16'-3"

Hall   Parlor
18'-6" x 18'-7"

Scale   0   5   10   15   20   25   30   35   40   45   Feet

Morris Jackson · Del·

VIEW FROM THE EAST
MONTGOMERY PLACE, BARRYTOWN, NEW YORK
Now owned by General John Ross Delafield

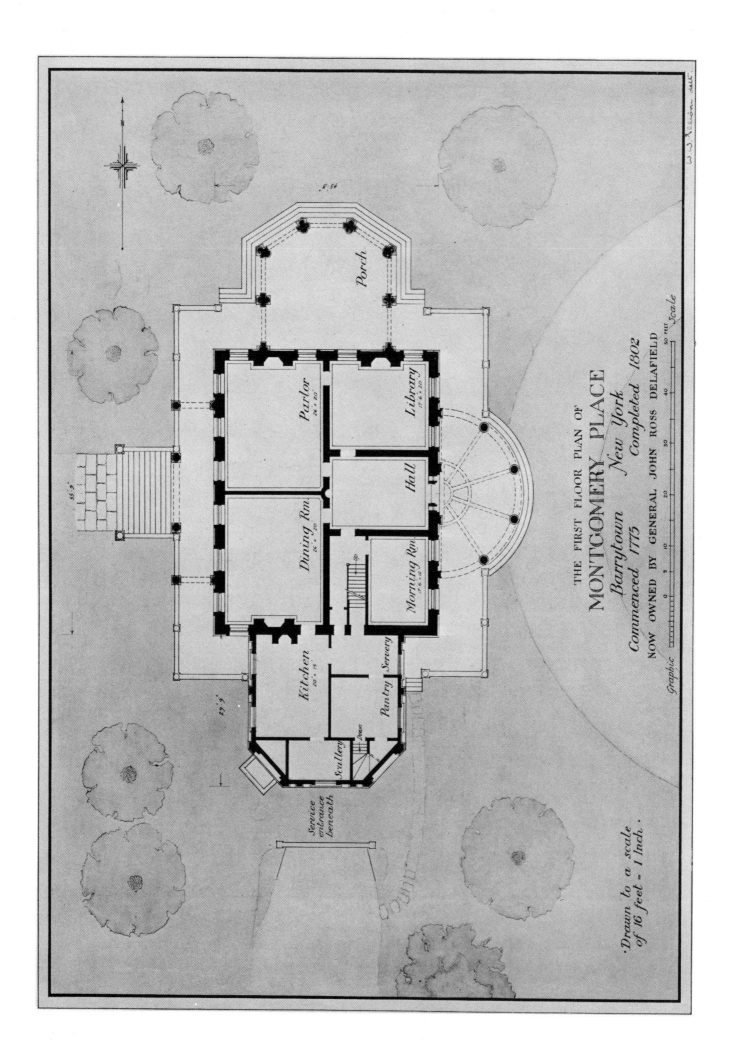

THE FIRST FLOOR PLAN OF
MONTGOMERY PLACE
Barrytown   New York
Commenced   1775   Completed   1802
NOW OWNED BY GENERAL JOHN ROSS DELAFIELD

Porch

Parlor
26' x 20'

Library
17'6" x 20'

Dining Rm.
26' x 20'

Hall

Morning Rm.
17'6" x 12'

Kitchen
20' x 18'

Pantry Servery

Scullery

Door

Service
entrance
beneath

Graphic

Scale

·Drawn to a scale
of 16 feet = 1 Inch.

East Facade

MONTGOMERY PLACE

at Barrytown, N.Y.

Drawn to a scale of ¹/₁₆ inch=1'-0"   Graphic |■■■■■ 0 5 10 15 20 25| Scale

G. A. Maag

THE NORTH PORCH

MONTGOMERY PLACE, BARRYTOWN, NEW YORK

South End of the South Wing

MONTGOMERY PLACE, BARRYTOWN, NEW YORK

PART OF EAST FAÇADE

MONTGOMERY PLACE
Barrytown · New York ·

·Graphic Scale·

Servants
Parlor
9'6"×13'0"   Hall

Servants
Dining Room

Porch

Servants
Kitchen   Pantry

Kitchen
16'10"×17'0"

Conservatory
15'6"×17'10"

Dining
Room
14'8"×27'4"

Flower
Room

Pantry

Lift

Library
9'6"×18'0"

Morning Room
8'2"×10'8"

Grand Stair Hall
12'2"×27'9"

up

dn
up

Entrance Alcove

Second Parlor
17'6"×20'3"

First Parlor
17'6"×20'4"

Porch

N

THE ALSOP HOUSE
301 High Street Middletown Connecticut
Erected in 1839
ARCHITECT unknown BUILDER unknown
Graphic scale 0 5 10   1/16"=1'-0" actual scale

H. Watkins Del.

195

THE ALSOP HOUSE, MIDDLETOWN, CONNECTICUT

N. Watkins Del.

The original frescoes of
niches, sculpture and urns
shown above are a rare form
of decoration in this country

THE ALSOP HOUSE
301 High Street Middletown Connecticut
Graphic scale 1/8"= 1' o" actual scale

THE FIRST PARLOR

THE ALSOP HOUSE, MIDDLETOWN, CONNECTICUT

The original painted decorations, curtain rods, mantel garniture, and mirrors
are fine examples of the Empire style

The Chippendale Gate

THE COWLES HOUSE, OLD GATE, FARMINGTON, CONNECTICUT

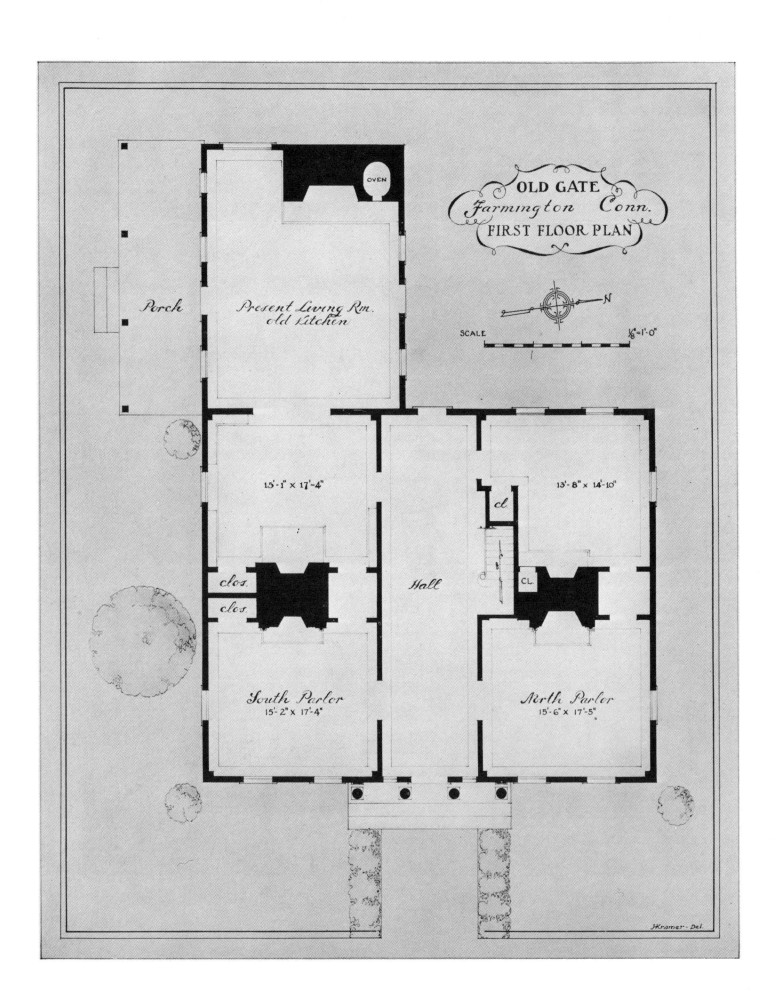

Porch

Present Living Rm.
old Kitchen

OVEN

OLD GATE
Farmington Conn.
FIRST FLOOR PLAN

SCALE ⅛"=1'-0"

N

15'-1" × 17'-4"

13'-8" × 14'-10"

cl.

clos.

CL.

clos.

Hall

South Parlor
15'-2" × 17'-4"

North Parlor
15'-6" × 17'-5"

J. Kramer - Del.

200

THE EAST FAÇADE

THE COWLES HOUSE, OLD GATE, FARMINGTON, CONNECTICUT

OLD GATE
Farmington, Connecticut.

ORIGINAL WING *was built by the* REV. SAMUEL HOOKER *in the year* 1660
MAIN HOUSE *was built by* CAPT. SOLOMON COWLES *in* 1781
with BRITISH PRISONERS *from* NEWGATE PRISON
LATER ADDITIONS *made in* 1900 *by* ADMIRAL WM. SHEFFIELD COWLES
and MRS. COWLES [ANNA ROOSEVELT]

Scale ⅛ inch equals 1 foot.

H.Kramer. Del.

"OLD GATE"
Farmington, Connecticut.

ORIGINAL WING was built by the REV. SAMUEL HOOKER in the year 1660

MAIN HOUSE was built by CAPT. SOLOMON COWLES in 1781
with BRITISH PRISONERS from NEWGATE PRISON

LATER ADDITIONS made in 1900 by ADMIRAL WM. SHEFFIELD COWLES
and MRS COWLES [ANNA ROOSEVELT]

Scale ⅛ inch equals 1 foot.

JKramer Del.

View from the Southwest

View from the South

THE COWLES HOUSE, OLD GATE, FARMINGTON, CONNECTICUT

Scale ⊏⊐⊏⊐⊏⊐ ½" = 1'-0"

SOUTH PARLOR

OLD GATE

FARMINGTON

CONNECTICUT

THE OLD GATE

as it was before palings were removed and stone wall built.

H.Kramer Del.

THE GATE AND HOUSE FROM THE EAST

THE COWLES HOUSE, OLD GATE, FARMINGTON, CONNECTICUT

This House also Known as The King Hooper House
EAST
ELEVATION OF
"The Lindens"
DANVERS - ESSEX CO.
MASSACHUSETTS
House Built cir.
1754
Scale
One Inch Equals Sixteen Feet
Scale in Feet

THE LINDENS, BUILT IN DANVERS, MASSACHUSETTS

THE EAST FAÇADE

THE LINDENS, BUILT IN DANVERS, MASSACHUSETTS

Now removed, rebuilt in Washington, D. C., and owned by Mrs. George Maurice Morris. As it appears today

DANVERS
ESSEX COUNTY

MAIN ENTRANCE of
THE LINDENS
SCALE: ¼"=1'-0"

BUILT 1754
MASSACHUSETTS

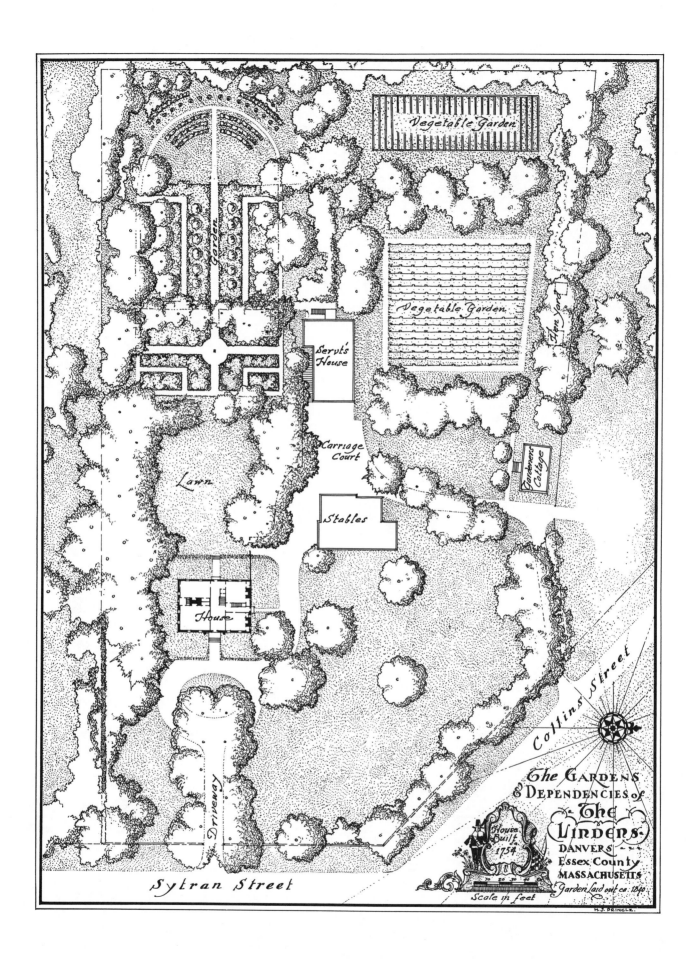

The Gardens & Dependencies of The Lindens
Danvers — Essex County MASSACHUSETTS
Garden laid out ca. 1840

House Built 1754

Scale in feet

M. J. Pringle.

Vegetable Garden

Vegetable Garden

Servt's House

Carriage Court

Stables

Gardener's Cottage

Lawn

House

Garden

The Yard

Driveway

Collins Street

Sylvan Street

THE WEST DOOR

THE LINDENS, BUILT IN DANVERS, MASSACHUSETTS

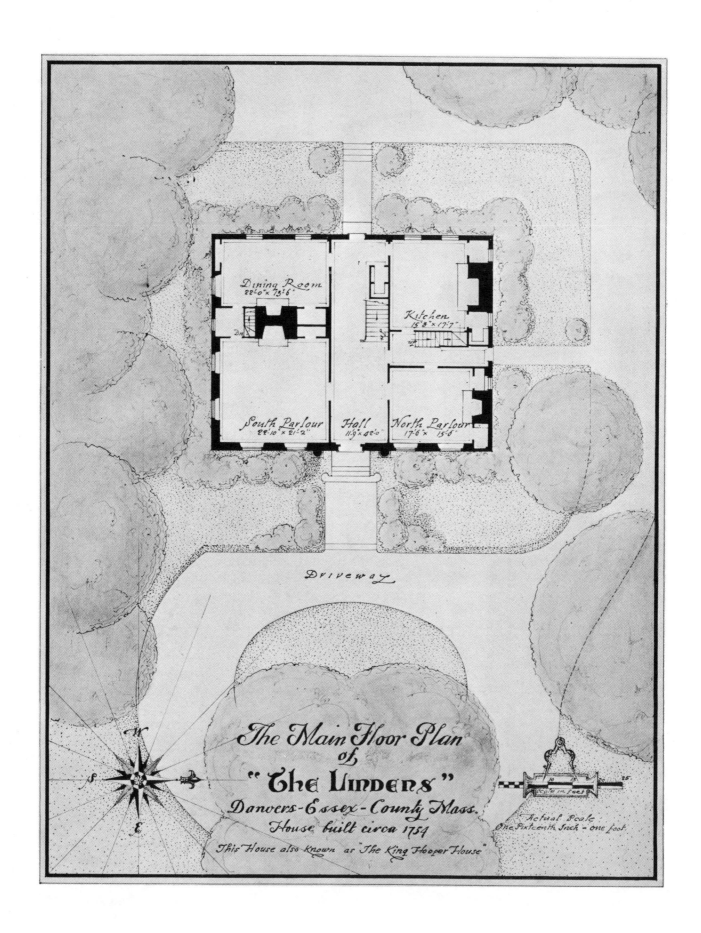

Dining Room
22'-0" x 15'-6"

Kitchen
15'-8" x 17'-7"

South Parlour
28'-10" x 21'-2"

Hall
11'-9" x 42'-0"

North Parlour
17'-6" x 15'-6"

Driveway

The Main Floor Plan
of
"The Lindens"
Danvers - Essex - County Mass.
House built circa 1754
This House also known as "The King Hooper House"

Actual Scale
One Sixteenth Inch = one foot

W   S   E

The Entrance Hall and Staircase

THE LINDENS, BUILT IN DANVERS, MASSACHUSETTS

The Main Hall

THE LINDENS, BUILT IN DANVERS, MASSACHUSETTS

Photograph by Frances Benjamin Johnston

The Dining Room

THE LINDENS, BUILT IN DANVERS, MASSACHUSETTS

The Drawing Room

As it stands in the art gallery in Kansas City

THE LINDENS, BUILT IN DANVERS, MASSACHUSETTS

THE DRAWING ROOM

As it stands in the art gallery in Kansas City

THE LINDENS, BUILT IN DANVERS, MASSACHUSETTS

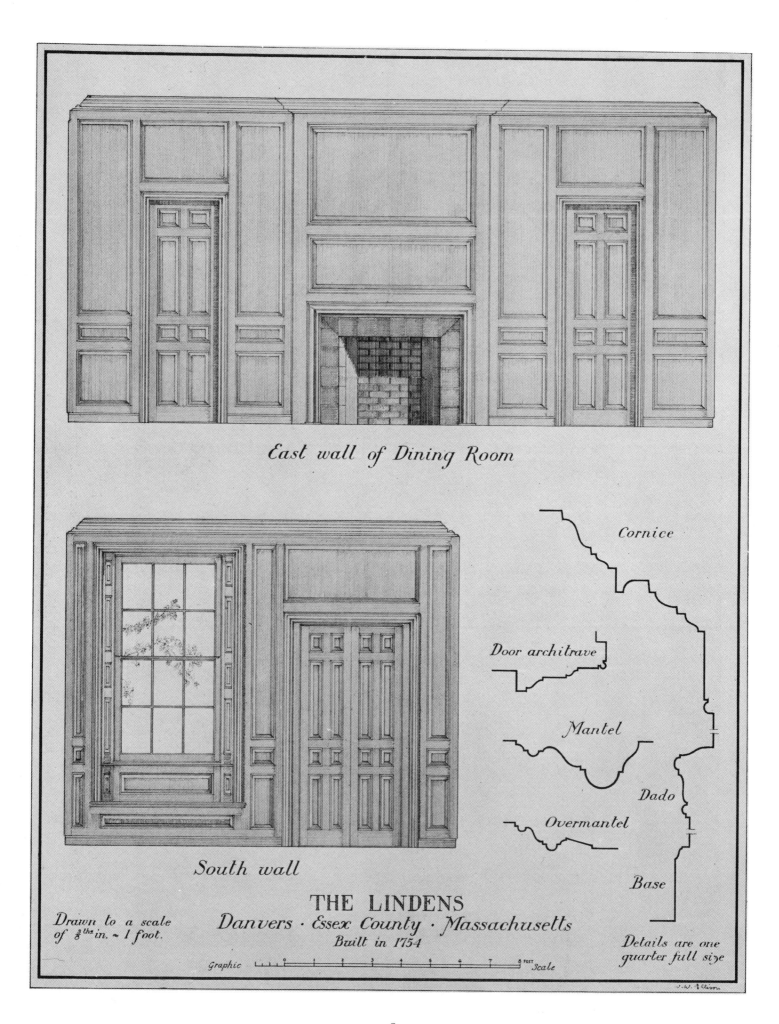

East wall of Dining Room

South wall

Cornice

Door architrave

Mantel

Overmantel

Dado

Base

THE LINDENS
Danvers · Essex County · Massachusetts
Built in 1754

Drawn to a scale
of ⅜ths in. ~ 1 foot.

Graphic   Scale

Details are one
quarter full size

THE STAIRCASE LANDING

THE LINDENS, BUILT IN DANVERS, MASSACHUSETTS

Photograph by Frances Benjamin Johnston

THE SITTING ROOM

THE LINDENS, BUILT IN DANVERS, MASSACHUSETTS

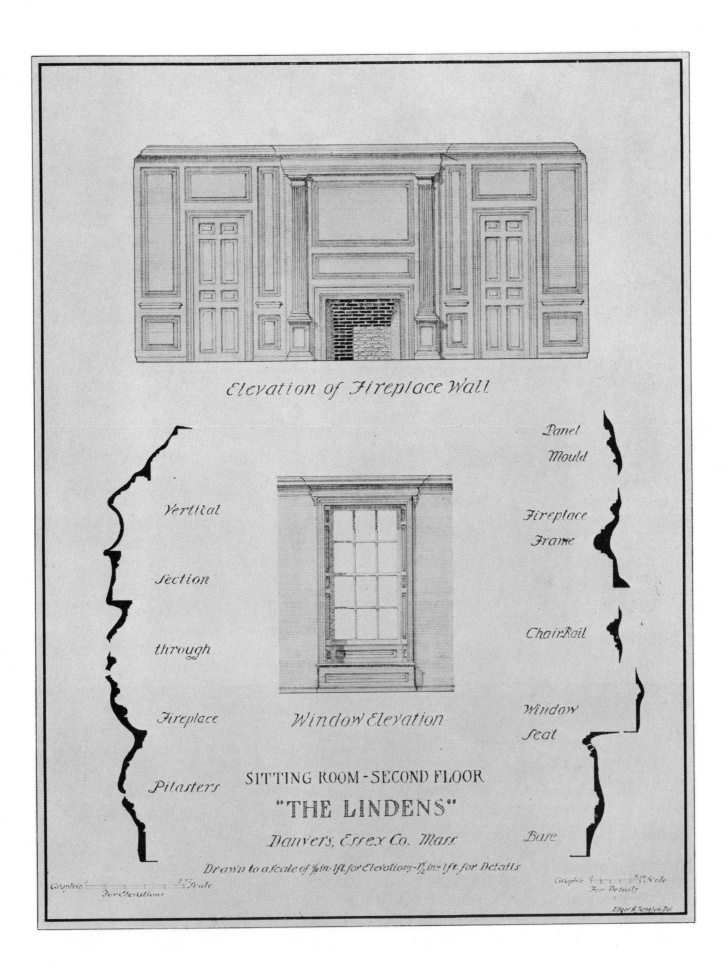

Elevation of Fireplace Wall

Panel
Mould

Vertical

Fireplace
Frame

Section

through

Chair Rail

Window Elevation

Fireplace

Window
Seat

Pilasters

SITTING ROOM – SECOND FLOOR
"THE LINDENS"
Danvers, Essex Co. Mass.

Base

Drawn to a scale of ½ in.= 1 ft. for Elevations – 1½ in.= 1 ft. for Details

Graphic —————— Scale
For Elevations

Graphic ——— No Scale
For Details

Edgar A. Josselyn, Del.

THE LINDENS,
BUILT IN
DANVERS,
MASSACHU-
SETTS

FLOOR DETAILS

Photographs by
Frances Benjamin Johnston

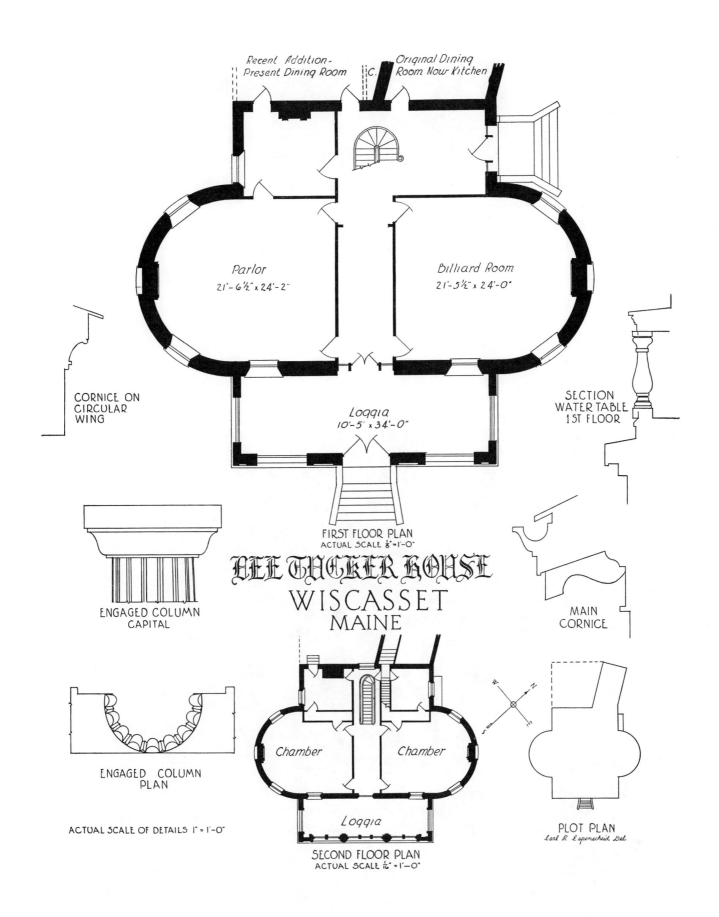

Recent Addition·
Present Dining Room

Original Dining
Room Now Kitchen

Parlor
21'-6½" x 24'-2"

Billiard Room
21'-5½" x 24'-0"

CORNICE ON
CIRCULAR
WING

Loggia
10'-5' x 34'-0"

SECTION
WATER TABLE
1ST FLOOR

FIRST FLOOR PLAN
ACTUAL SCALE ⅛"=1'-0"

LEE TUCKER HOUSE
WISCASSET
MAINE

ENGAGED COLUMN
CAPITAL

MAIN
CORNICE

ENGAGED COLUMN
PLAN

Chamber

Chamber

PLOT PLAN
Carl R Lapenscheid. Del.

ACTUAL SCALE OF DETAILS 1"=1'-0"

Loggia

SECOND FLOOR PLAN
ACTUAL SCALE 1/16"=1'-0"

LEE–TUCKER HOUSE, WISCASSET, MAINE

223

The South Front

LEE–TUCKER HOUSE, WISCASSET, MAINE

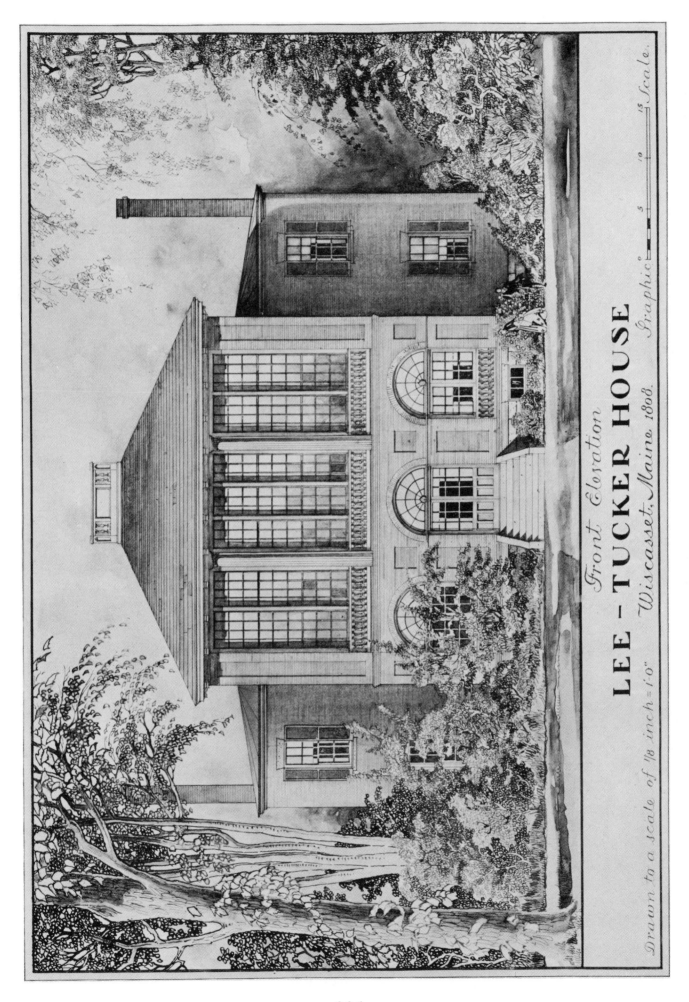

Front Elevation

LEE - TUCKER HOUSE
Wiscasset, Maine 1808.

Drawn to a scale of 1/8 inch = 1'0"   Graphic   Scale.

VIEW FROM THE EAST

LEE–TUCKER HOUSE, WISCASSET, MAINE

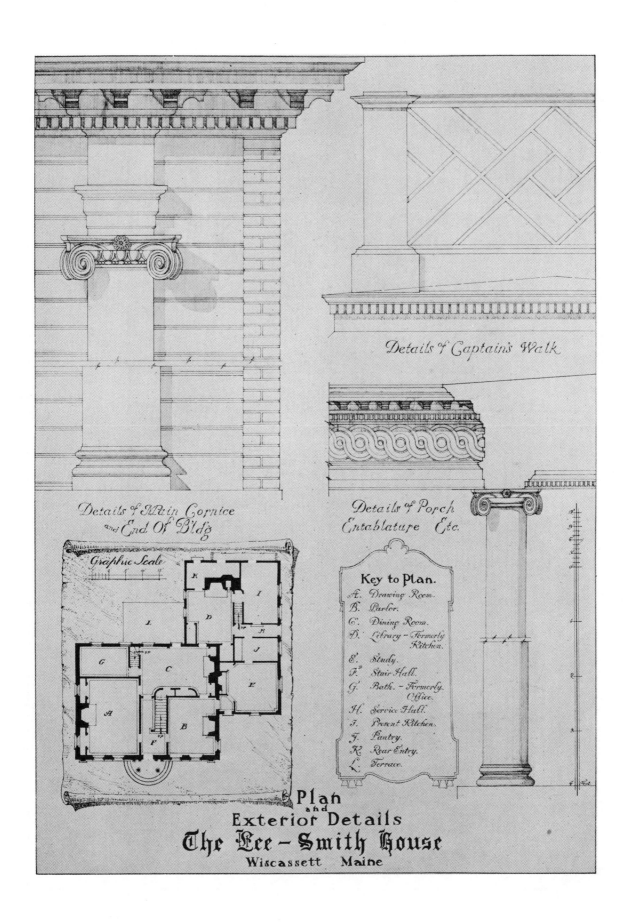

Details of Captain's Walk

Details of Main Cornice and End Of Bldg

Details of Porch Entablature Etc.

Graphic Scale

Key to Plan.
A. Drawing Room.
B. Parlor.
C. Dining Room.
D. Library – Formerly Kitchen.
E. Study.
F. Stair Hall.
G. Bath – Formerly Office.
H. Service Hall.
I. Present Kitchen.
J. Pantry.
K. Rear Entry.
L. Terrace.

Plan and Exterior Details
The Lee–Smith House
Wiscassett Maine

LEE–SMITH HOUSE, WISCASSET, MAINE

Entrance Facade.
"The Lee – Smith House." Wiscassett." Maine."
Built about 1792 by Silas Lee.
Later owned by Governor Samuel Smith.
And still in Possession of his Descendants.

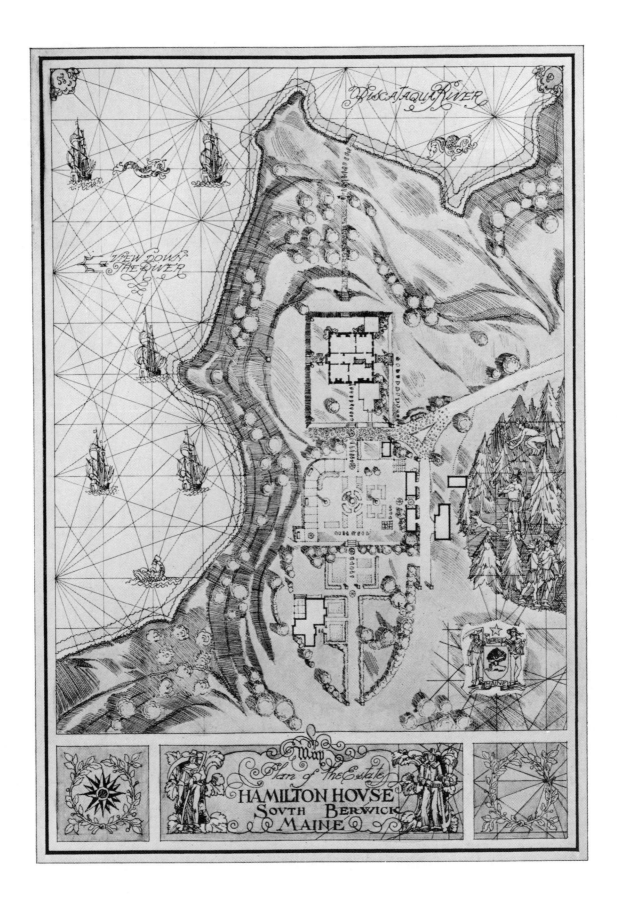

HAMILTON HOUSE, SOUTH BERWICK, MAINE

Now owned by Mrs. Henry Vaughan

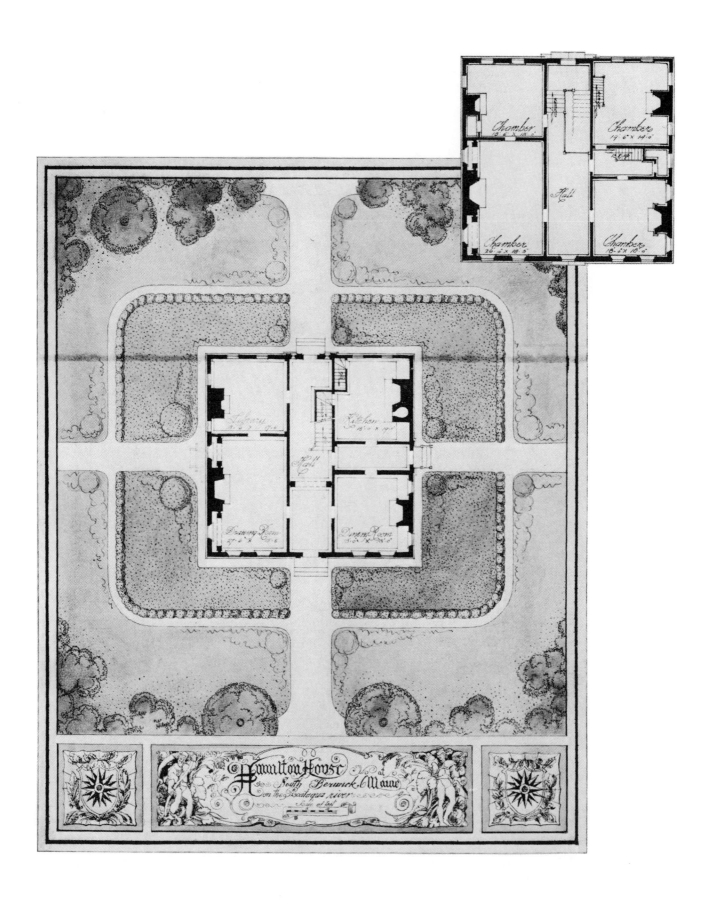

DIRIGO

FRONT VIEW
HAMILTON HOVSE
SOVTH BERWICK
MAINE
SCALE OF FEET

THE ENTRANCE FAÇADE

HAMILTON HOUSE, SOUTH BERWICK, MAINE

THE RIVER FRONT

HAMILTON HOUSE, SOUTH BERWICK, MAINE

The Entrance Hall

HAMILTON HOUSE, SOUTH BERWICK, MAINE

Showing its setting on the Piscataqua River

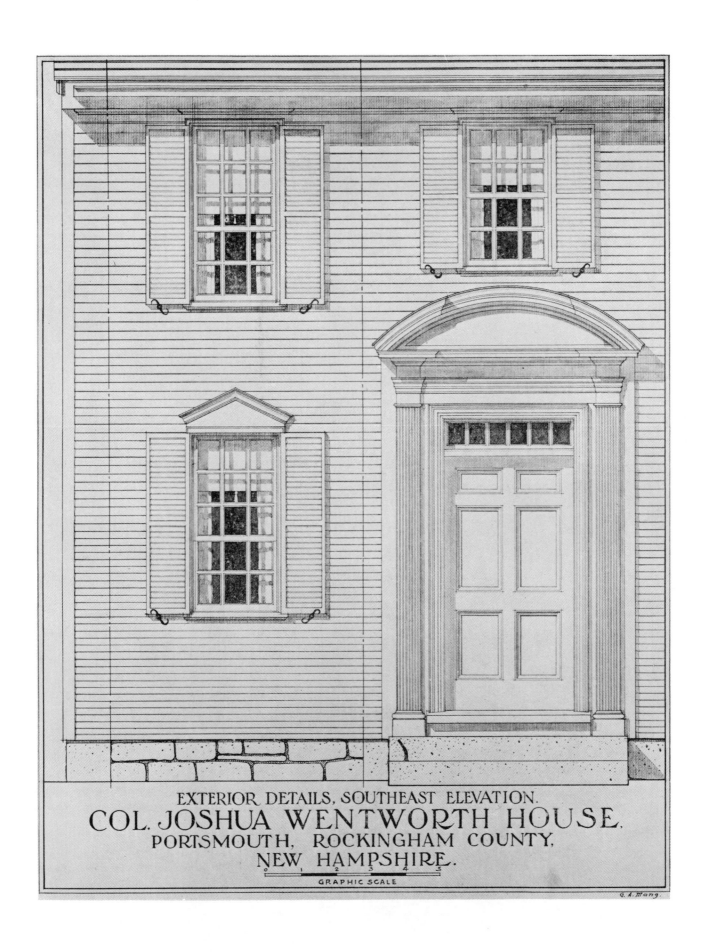

EXTERIOR DETAILS, SOUTHEAST ELEVATION.
COL. JOSHUA WENTWORTH HOUSE.
PORTSMOUTH, ROCKINGHAM COUNTY,
NEW HAMPSHIRE.

0 1 2 3 4 5
GRAPHIC SCALE

G. A. Mang.

THE COLONEL JOSHUA WENTWORTH HOUSE, PORTSMOUTH, NEW HAMPSHIRE

FRONT ELEVATION,
COL. JOSHUA WENTWORTH HOUSE.
PORTSMOUTH, NEW HAMPSHIRE. BUILT-1770.

GRAPHIC SCALE.

G. A. morg.

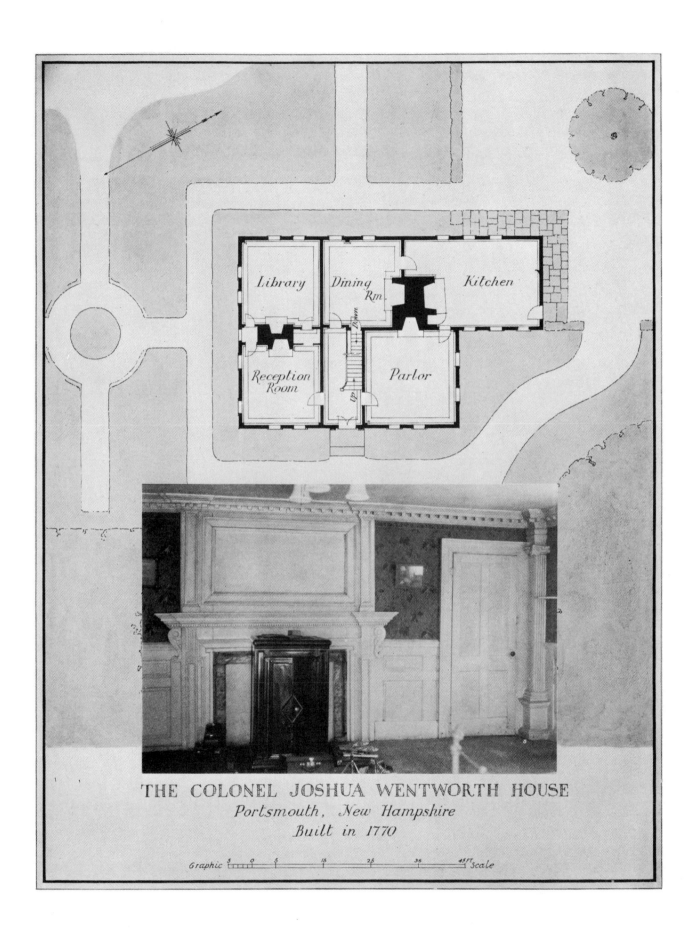

Library   Dining Rm.   Kitchen

Reception Room   Parlor

THE COLONEL JOSHUA WENTWORTH HOUSE
Portsmouth, New Hampshire
Built in 1770

Graphic   5   0   5   15   25   35   45 FT. Scale

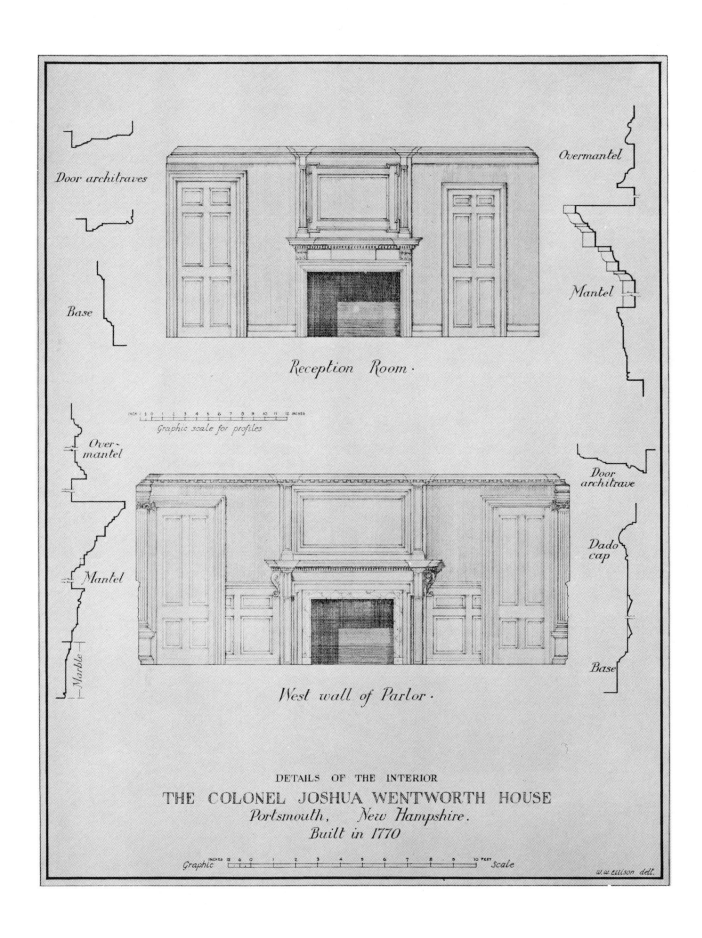

Door architraves

Base

Reception Room.

Overmantel

Mantel

Graphic scale for profiles

Over-mantel

Mantel

Marble

Door architrave

Dado cap

Base

West wall of Parlor.

DETAILS OF THE INTERIOR

THE COLONEL JOSHUA WENTWORTH HOUSE
Portsmouth, New Hampshire.
Built in 1770

Graphic Scale

w.w.ellison delt.

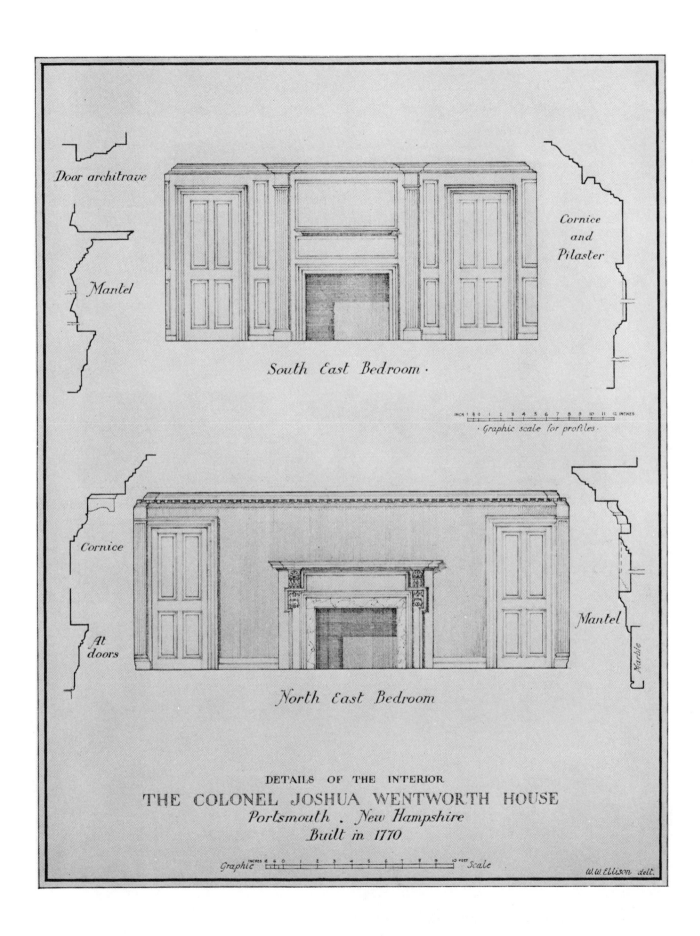

Door architrave

Mantel

Cornice
and
Pilaster

South East Bedroom.

INCH 1 8 0 1 2 3 4 5 6 7 8 9 10 11 12 INCHES
· Graphic scale for profiles ·

Cornice

At
doors

Mantel

Marble

North East Bedroom

DETAILS OF THE INTERIOR

THE COLONEL JOSHUA WENTWORTH HOUSE
Portsmouth . New Hampshire
Built in 1770

Graphic INCHES 12 6 0 1 2 3 4 5 6 7 8 9 10 FEET Scale

W.W.Ellison delt.

Mantel Detail

Mantel Detail

THE COLONEL JOSHUA WENTWORTH HOUSE, PORTSMOUTH, NEW HAMPSHIRE

240

VIEW FROM THE STREET

THE JOHN BROWN HOUSE (1786), PROVIDENCE, RHODE ISLAND

View of the Entrance Façade

THE JOHN BROWN HOUSE, PROVIDENCE, RHODE ISLAND

Courtesy of the Monograph Series.   Photograph by Arthur C. Haskell

VIEW OF THE SIDE

THE JOHN BROWN HOUSE, PROVIDENCE, RHODE ISLAND

Courtesy of the Monograph Series. Photograph by Arthur C. Haskell

THE ENTRANCE PORCH

THE JOHN BROWN HOUSE, PROVIDENCE, RHODE ISLAND

DETAIL OF ENTRANCE DOOR

THE JOHN BROWN HOUSE, PROVIDENCE, RHODE ISLAND

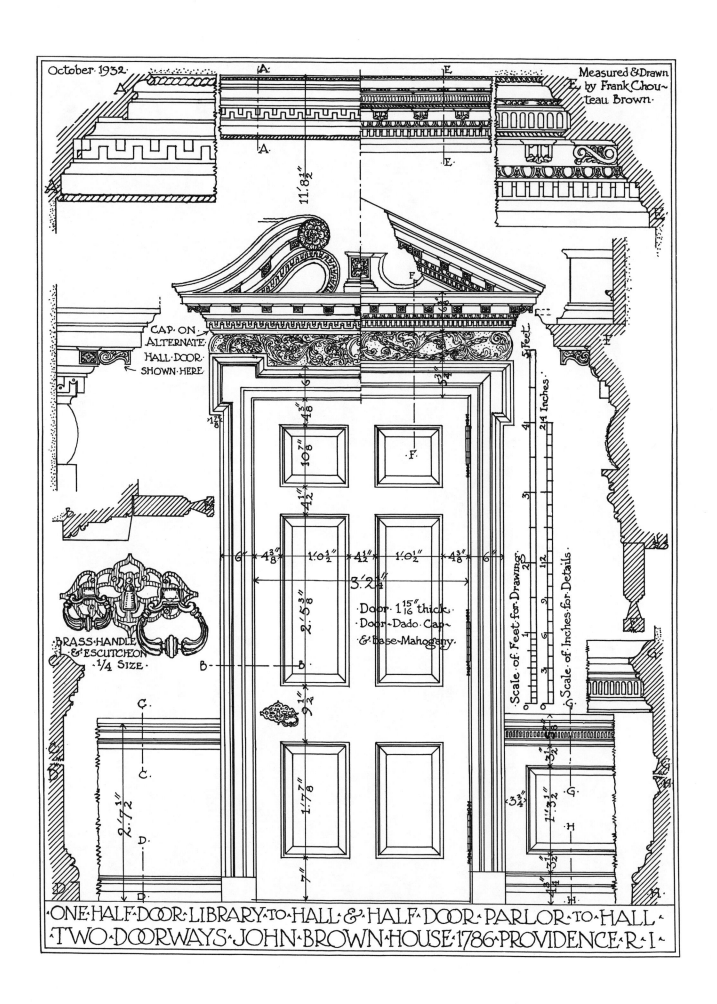

October 1932

Measured & Drawn by Frank Chouteau Brown.

CAP ON ALTERNATE HALL DOOR SHOWN HERE

BRASS HANDLE & ESCUTCHEON 1/4 SIZE

Door 1 15/16" thick.
Door-Dado-Cap-
& Base-Mahogany.

Scale of Feet for Drawing.

Scale of Inches for Details.

5 Feet

24 Inches

ONE·HALF·DOOR·LIBRARY·TO·HALL·&·HALF·DOOR·PARLOR·TO·HALL·
TWO·DOORWAYS·JOHN·BROWN·HOUSE·1786·PROVIDENCE·R·I·

Courtesy of the Monograph Series. Photograph by Arthur C. Haskell

DETAIL OF THE LIBRARY DOORWAY

THE JOHN BROWN HOUSE, PROVIDENCE, RHODE ISLAND

Courtesy of the Monograph Series. Photograph by Arthur C. Haskell

DETAIL OF CORNICE AND PEDIMENTAL OVERDOOR, THE PARLOR

THE JOHN BROWN HOUSE, PROVIDENCE, RHODE ISLAND

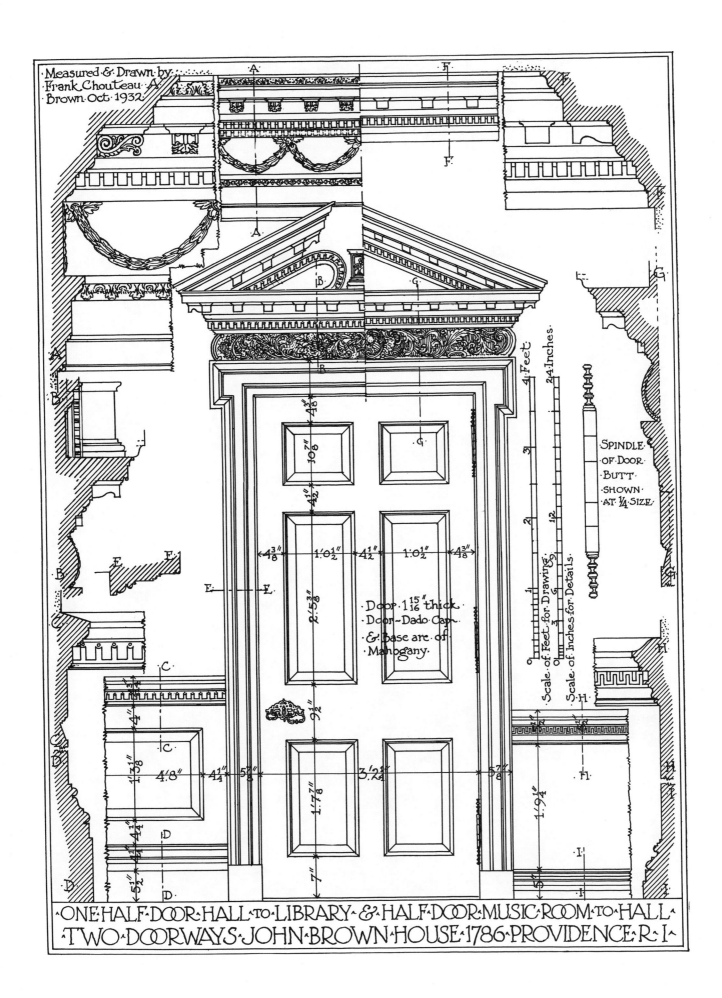

Measured & Drawn by
Frank Chouteau
Brown. Oct. 1932.

SPINDLE
·OF·DOOR·
·BUTT·
·SHOWN·
·AT·¼·SIZE·

·Door·1 15/16"·thick·
·Door~Dado·Cap·
·& base·are·of·
·Mahogany·

·ONE·HALF·DOOR·HALL·TO·LIBRARY·&·HALF·DOOR·MUSIC·ROOM·TO·HALL·
·TWO·DOORWAYS·JOHN·BROWN·HOUSE·1786·PROVIDENCE·R·I·

249

Courtesy of the Monograph Series. Photograph by Arthur C. Haskell

DOORWAY, THE MUSIC ROOM

THE JOHN BROWN HOUSE, PROVIDENCE, RHODE ISLAND

The

Samuel Forman

House

Syracuse ~ New York

Built in 1812

Graphic Scale

First Floor Plan
Graphic Scale

Bed Room
10'-0" x 8'-0"

Dining Room
17'-6" x 16'-0"

Bed Room
10'-0" x 8'-0"

Parlor
17'-11" x 16'-1"

Hall
17'-10" x 10'-6"

FRANK J. BRINCE DEL.

THE SAMUEL FORMAN HOUSE, SYRACUSE, NEW YORK

The Front Entrance

THE SAMUEL FORMAN HOUSE, SYRACUSE, NEW YORK

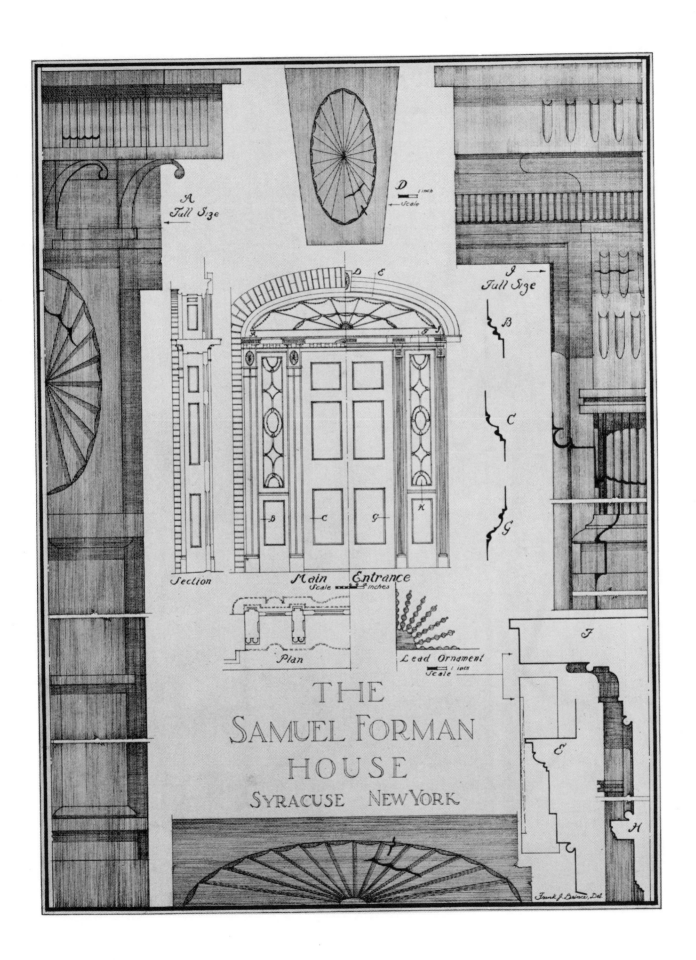

A
Full Size

D
1 inch
Scale

I
Full Size

B

C

G

Section

Main Entrance
Scale

Plan

Lead Ornament
Scale

F

E

H

THE
SAMUEL FORMAN
HOUSE
SYRACUSE NEW YORK

Frank J. Bruce, Del.

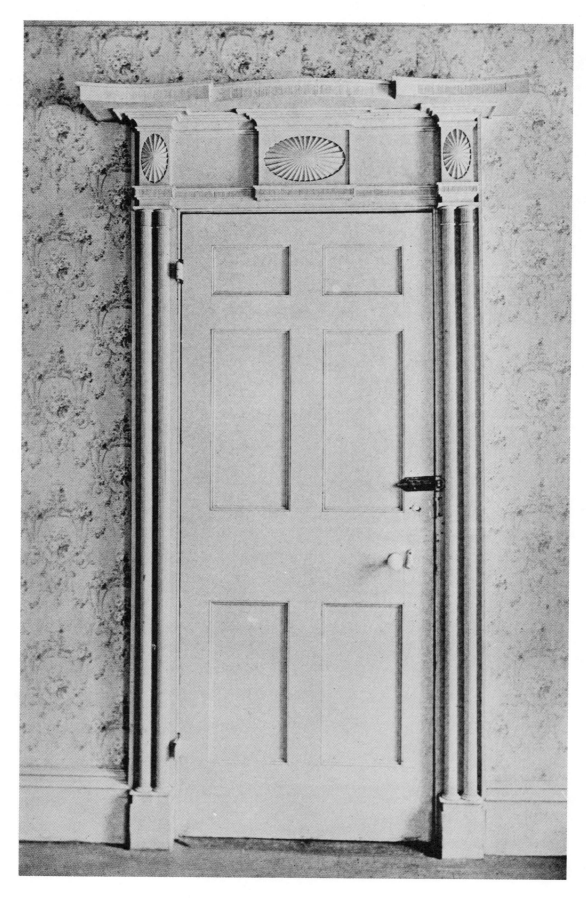

PARLOR DOOR

THE SAMUEL FORMAN HOUSE, SYRACUSE, NEW YORK

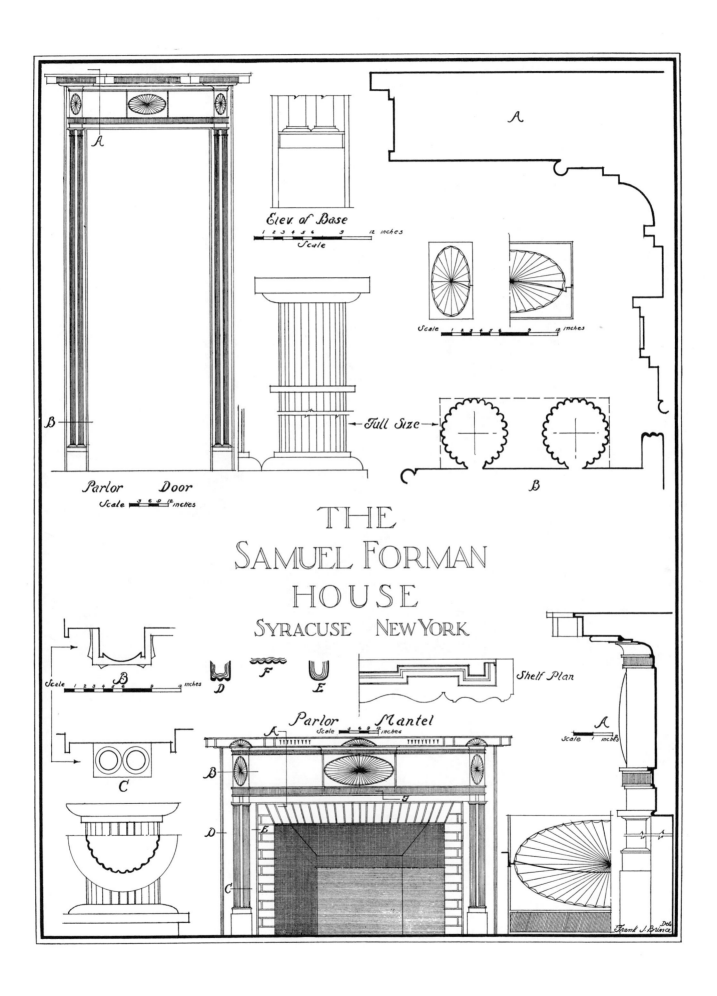

Elev. of Base

1 2 3 4 5 6 · · · 9 · · · 12 inches
Scale

Scale 1 2 3 4 5 6 · · · 9 · · · 12 inches

← Full Size →

Parlor Door

Scale · 3 6 9 12 inches

THE
SAMUEL FORMAN
HOUSE
SYRACUSE NEW YORK

Scale 1 2 3 4 5 6 · · · 9 · · · inches

Shelf Plan

Parlor Mantel

Scale · 3 6 9 12 inches

Scale 1 inches

Del.
Frank J. Prince

255

The Front Elevation

THE SAMUEL FORMAN HOUSE, SYRACUSE, NEW YORK